BLACK COUNTRY TO RED CHINA

Esther Cheo Ying was born in Shanghai in 1932. From the age of six she spent her childhood in England but returned to China at seventeen. In the Chinese People's Liberation Army, then in the New China News Agency and on Peking Radio, she saw the New China in the making – from the inside.

Eleven years later she returned to Britain and became a teacher. For many years until retirement she was head of a primary school in the West Country. She and her journalist husband then moved back to the outskirts of London to be near their children and grandchildren. Her hobbies include sculpture, writing and walking and her daughter Polly is a successful author.

ESTHER CHEO YING

Black Country to Red China

One girl's story from war-torn England to
Revolutionary China

VINTAGE BOOKS
London

Published by Vintage 2009

2 4 6 8 10 9 7 5 3 1

Copyright © Esther Samson 1980

Esther Samson has asserted her right under the Copyright, Designs and Patents Act 1988 to be identified as the author of this work

First published in Great Britain in 1980 by Hutchinson

Vintage
Random House, 20 Vauxhall Bridge Road,
London SW1V 2SA

www.vintage-books.co.uk

Addresses for companies within The Random House Group Limited can be found at: www.randomhouse.co.uk/offices.htm

The Random House Group Limited Reg. No. 954009

A CIP catalogue record for this book
is available from the British Library

ISBN 9780099536031

The Random House Group Limited supports The Forest Stewardship Council (FSC), the leading international forest certification organisation. All our titles that are printed on Greenpeace approved FSC certified paper carry the FSC logo. Our paper procurement policy can be found at: www.rbooks.co.uk/environment

Mixed Sources
Product group from well-managed forests and other controlled sources
www.fsc.org Cert no. TT-COC-2139
© 1996 Forest Stewardship Council

Printed and bound in Great Britain by
CPI Cox & Wyman, Reading, RG1 8EX

Contents

Illustrations

Preface

When I wrote this book, the Cultural Revolution was not long past. So I restrained myself in part. I did not want to reopen old scars or unwittingly cause harm to people who had already suffered so much. The incidents in the book are true, but in some cases I have changed names, places and circumstances. What I tell is as I saw it and felt it. I have exercised restraint in consideration of others' feelings, but I realize that in recalling the events of my life I am likely to upset some friends and relations – East and West. I regret that I cannot tell my story without some people feeling hurt.

I prefaced my story when it was published in 1980 with the following words:

'The events of this book took place thirty years ago when, like so many rebels of the postwar years, I searched and thought there was a solution to all social problems.

I dedicate the book to my foster-mother "Auntie Dash", who helped to form my mind so that it could question the eastern and western philosophies and gave me the courage to make the right decisions and stand by them.'

Now seven years on, I have just returned from my first visit to China nearly three decades after the events recounted here. I met again many old friends and comrades – and realize that to complete the picture my dedication should include them. Not by individual names – that would be invidious. They all suffered severely during the Cultural Revolution and the run-up to it but their attitude to those bitter years is mainly philosophical. One of them, himself now seriously incapacitated as a result of his treatment by the Red Guards, even felt able to say: 'At least it cleared the air.'

He added: 'Write another book now that you have come back and seen how China has changed.'

I intend to do that. But meanwhile it was cheering to find that so many of the judgements I made in this book are now widely shared in China. 'You were right', said some of those who thirty years ago were foremost in castigating my 'political mistakes'. Of course it was pleasing to receive acknowledgements that I was right – even if I was right at the 'wrong' time. But my colleagues and friends of those years stayed on. Those people, some now dead, battled on to bring closer the ideals which had first taken me to China. I learned much from them – and despite them. So in part this book should be dedicated to them.

As for my Chinese family, that is another story. It was only through a chance remark by a visitor to London from Peking three years ago that I learned that my father – the other main reason for my original return to China – had died in 1961.

It took until April this year to find and meet my half-sister and four half-brothers.

Once I had left China when they were youngsters, the limited protection that my status in Peking may have afforded them was gone. My sister achieved her ambition to become a doctor, but the boys were prevented from entering university and under the political suppression which culminated in that nightmare decade of the Red Guards they were forced for years to labour on the land in harsh parts of China thousands of miles remote from their home city, Shanghai.

Theirs is a story of great suffering and bitterness which did not end until years after the death of Mao Tse-tung and the downfall of his wife.

Twelve years after Father's death, a Shanghai court finally cleared him of all the counter-revolutionary charges for which he had been sentenced. When I learned this, I cried. All the suffering heaped on his Shanghai family – and incidentally on me – based on trumped-up charges. All the hardships undergone by my sister and brothers based on simple injustice – for unlike most of my Peking friends and colleagues, my Shanghai family were 'non-political', not cadres, just wanting a normal, straightforward life. Faced with their pent up feelings, it is hard to stay objective and see China for what it has become

– a great nation of wonderfully resilient people.

May their optimism for the future be justified – and may my father's tortured soul at last rest in peace.

Esther Cheo Ying
Devon
June 1987

1

Return to China

I stepped down the gang-plank in Tientsin Harbour, dirty and dishevelled, and managed to place myself in the middle of a group of young Chinese students to pass the Communist guards as they cursorily glanced at the people moving along with their bundles.

It was February 1949. I was seventeen. I had left the post-war gloom and depression of England and the English half of my family to return to China, which I had not seen since I was six years old. The world was just becoming aware of the advances of the Chinese Red Army. Tientsin, one of China's main northern ports, had been taken. I had been in Hong-kong for several weeks waiting for Tientsin to be 'liberated' by the Red Army so that I could smuggle up by sea to join them. Central and South China were still in the hands of the Nationalists, and somewhere in Shanghai lived my Chinese father.

The only Chinese words I knew were my name. Anyone taking a close look could see that my features were not completely oriental despite the blue cotton Chinese dress and cropped black hair whose colour fortunately I had inherited from the Chinese side of the family.

As I moved along the busy Tientsin port on to the dusty streets accompanied by myriad voices of unintelligible chatter, I thought of what my English foster parents, 'Auntie' and 'Uncle', would say if they could see me. Living with them back in Staffordshire, I was a regular attender at chapel and sang solo at the Methodist anniversaries where the congregation came to hear Mrs Colley's ''vacuee Chink'. As I sang their heavenly music I would look at the simpering smiling faces and dream of this very day – back in China – when I could leave all that poverty, those fish-belly-white skins of that coal-mining village and return to the country where I had been born.

It had taken two weeks to sail from Hongkong to Tientsin as a deck passenger on a small cargo boat. I had joined a group of Chinese graduates from England, all eager to serve the New China. There should also have been Don, my Chinese husband of a few months – Captain Cheng Tung-yung of the Chinese air force. But he had gone to Canton instead, to see which side was likely to win in this civil war between Communists and Nationalists. There was a Ph.D from Oxford; a Chinese Professor of Linguistics; scientists; and a steel specialist from Sheffield who, as an underground Chinese Communist Party member, had come to England, studied and recruited fellow Chinese students. Two weeks earlier I had shuffled up the gang-plank in Hongkong, my head bent low, partially hidden by my bedding roll, in this group of Chinese students. We went as deck passengers because there was no other way for Chinese to reach the liberated areas of the North. We rolled out our bedding on the floor of the deck, then watched from the rails the coolies labouring under huge burdens as they rhythmically climbed up the gangplank. Every now and then a British officer rained blows on some wretch's head with a short truncheon. I watched, not daring to utter a word because my English voice might raise a few eyebrows, putting my journey in jeopardy. Suddenly one of the coolies dropped his load and turned round. The officer, surprised, took a step back, then the other coolies surrounded him. The passengers began to shout encouragement and in the heat of the moment I screamed out, 'Throw him overboard!' The officer turned a startled face up towards the deck-rails while my friends pulled me down. The coolies were now beginning to jostle him and make threatening gestures; another officer appeared and tried in Cantonese to make himself heard above the din. The noise and shouting was deafening. He disappeared and promptly returned with a trumpet which he flourished as if leading a charge and played a bar from *William Tell*. There was a surprised hush. He pacified the angry men with a promise that the now terrified fellow officer would be dealt with. For those present it was a turning point in East–West relationships. It gave a terrific morale boost to the Chinese passengers, who returned to their bedding rolls excitedly chatting with broad grins on their normally phlegmatic faces.

We had to lie low and stay quiet as we passed through the Taiwan Straits. Rumour had it that the Kuomintang, the Nationalists, had often stopped boats, discovered would-be revolutionaries on their way to join the enemy and thrown them overboard to the sharks. There were about 200 men and women sleeping rough on the deck. Each of us had a tiny sleeping space with just enough room to step through to the elementary lavatories, wooden buckets separated from us by a dirty piece of matting. Privacy was guaranteed by loud clearing of throats as a hand cautiously shook the matting and we called out, '*Yo Jen*' (Somebody here). During the day it was hot and stuffy behind the canvas awnings but marvellously cool and fresh at nights when we pulled back the canvas and breathed clear sea air.

Often during those sleepless nights on board the little cargo boat I had sweated with apprehension and heat. I thought of those I had left behind me and wondered why I did not feel sadness at the break. I felt unmoved even about parting from my Chinese husband, Don, whom I had married in England, only to leave him after three months because he refused to come with me. He had let me down after so many promises of life in a New China coloured by the thought that after so many years of pining and homesickness for my Chinese family and finding my roots again I would be able to be myself, instead of a half-Chinese lost soul in a country I had never been able to accept as my own. Now Don was somewhere in Nationalist China and I had thrown in my lot with these near-strangers with whom the only thing I had in common was the desire to become a member of the Communist revolutionary forces.

My English mother had been a chambermaid in the hotel where my father lodged while a student at the London School of Economics. She was a typical Cockney girl from Poplar. Her father was a brewer's drayman. She was seventeen, blonde and pretty. In the memoirs he sent me later, my father wrote that he took my mother out to dinner as a reward for

11

finding a ring he had lost. But I think that may have been a bit of romanticism on his part. He was a most romantic man and in 1931 they were married at a register office. Her father set off in pursuit in true Alfred Doolittle style, and they ran away to France where they boarded a ship for Shanghai, China.

It could not have been easy for my working-class mother to understand what marrying a Chinese Mandarin's son entailed. She was too young to understand and too ignorant of the different cultures of East and West to try to conform even a little to the customs of Chinese life. My father's family ostracized him for marrying a 'foreign devil'. The odds were too great for either of these two young people to try to make the marriage work. He was a brilliant only son of a rich magistrate from Szechuan Province in West China and had won a scholarship to study in England. Somewhere in his ancestry a grandmother had been a Persian slave brought along the silk route into China. He had large eyes and an aquiline nose, unusual characteristics in a Chinese. He took a teaching job in Shanghai and struggled to make ends meet. She had lost her nationality and, by British law then, was a Chinese subject, spurned by my father's Chinese family as a yellow-haired Barbarian and treated with contempt by the British community for marrying a Chinese.

I was born in January 1932, during a time of floods and famine, and a sister followed a year later. My father 'bought' a nurse. Ni Noo my new amah had given birth to twin girls which had been thrown behind a bush to die, while she came into the city to sell her milk. She spoiled and petted me, making me into a bad-tempered angry little girl whom no one could handle except her. I can remember kicking her in a fury, because she refused to buy me a live crocodile I saw in the market. On me she poured all the loving care that should have belonged to her starved twin daughters. In effect this illiterate peasant woman became my mother and laid the foundation, so important in early childhood, which was to influence me for the rest of my life and build up the urge during my years in England to return to the land of my birth. There are blank spaces in the memory of my childhood and of Ni Noo. I was told the parting was traumatic and it seems as if nature was kind and wiped most of it from my mind. My father wrote years later that she ripped her clothes off and tore the flesh from her breasts in a frenzy of despair as my mother dragged me away screaming on to the English ship. I can only remember a little of mother in those Shanghai days, but my father's memory stands out very clearly. There were secret trips on which he used to take me to visit my Chinese relatives. All I remember of my mother at that time were the fleeting moments of a golden-haired lady who insisted I called her auntie, a quick kiss and a promise of a present if I was good.

My brother was born during the Japanese invasion of Shanghai in 1936, and I can remember sitting in a car with a British policeman standing on one running board and a Japanese soldier on the other as we drove slowly through the Chinese quarters from the International Settlement where we lived and saw piles of dead and dying bodies, in order to take my desperately ill baby brother to the French Hospital.

By 1938 the situation in Shanghai was getting tense. British families were leaving on special ships sent by the government. My mother and her three children were not eligible. We were Chinese citizens. Relations between my parents had worsened, the only thing left to battle over were their three children. In Chinese law my father had every legal right to take us away and disown my mother. My sister and I were too bewildered to know to whom we belonged, except that during one quarrel I clung to Ni Noo while my father bribed my sister to come over to his side by making her a present of his red and blue marking pencil. My mother held my baby brother whom she adored. I wept in Ni Noo's arms because I so badly wanted that red and blue pencil. My mother's position was fraught with danger and for the first time since she ran away from home she wrote to my English grandfather and begged him to help her. He contacted his local MP, Clement Attlee, to enlist his help in getting my mother and us three children back to England. My mother's family had always been staunch Labour supporters and one of the first English verses my mother ever taught us in Shanghai was a Labour election jingle she used to sing. My sister and I would tramp around the courtyard singing in our squeaky Chinese voices:

'Vote Vote Vote for Mr Attlee, Punch old————— in the Jaw,
    If it wasn't for the King, we would do the bugger in,
            and he won't go voting any more. . . .'

Attlee, a compassionate man, made arrangements to get
my mother and her three children home to England. The
acting British Consul, much to his disgust, had to swallow his
contempt for my mother and give her a British passport. He
was a most unsympathetic man who was said to have had a
Japanese mistress and who apparently tried to salve his own
self-loathing in condemning my poor mother.

My father saw us off on a British boat packed with fleeing
refugees. He stayed on in Shanghai and soon succumbed to
the temptation of becoming rich. He prospered during the
Japanese occupation and when the war was over became even
more prosperous under the Nationalists when he became a
colonel in their army. He married a beautiful Chinese actress
and had many children. In the meantime my mother arrived
in England as the Second World War was declared. In using
the might of the British Empire and the services of Clement
Attlee she had succeeded in leaving my father powerless even
as a Chinese in his own country to have control over his children. The outbreak of the war made it easy to break all
contact with his now English family. And when rumours
reached him that we had all been killed in an air raid he
mourned and forgot.

When we arrived in London, my mother's family did not
want to be responsible for three half-Chinese children. She
tramped the streets, homeless, dragging three whining miserable children behind her. We stayed in a Salvation Army
Hostel for a few nights, and I can remember old, old people,
chipped enamel mugs of weak tea, prunes and watery
custard, thick hunks of bread and dripping and my sister
wetting herself because I could not take down the black iron
side of the cot to help her out. I did not know where my
mother had gone.

My next memory was of Dr Barnardo's Home, the coldness
of the people, the bad food, the lack of warmth and affection
and the strange language. We only knew a few words of

English and it was no use crying for the comforting arms of Ni Noo. 'Who is this Ni Noo? Be quiet and go to sleep. You will wake the others. Your father is dead. The sooner you know your place the better, my lady!'

Then came separation from my sister and brother as we were evacuated from the home during the panic of threatened German invasions and air raids and placed in different foster homes, then another foster home and another until I lost count of the number of homes I lived in. Bad homes, good homes, but all poor miners' homes in the Black Country of Staffordshire where the billeting money each foster child brought in was an important supplement to the family's income. With each bombardment of psychological shock I became more and more withdrawn, stopped crying and withdrew into the safety of a shell and lived in a fantasy world in which Ni Noo and my father were the only inhabitants. By the time I came to my final foster home with 'Auntie' and 'Uncle' the change was completed. I was nine years old and had completely shut myself in from the ugly surroundings, and the attempts of 'Uncle' and 'Auntie' to draw some response from me. During the war years as an evacuee 'half-caste' in the Midlands I dreamed of the day when we could all be a family again. In my childish mind it was the war that broke our family up. My parents' bitter quarrels and fights were unimportant. I could soon settle that by giving them each a cigarette and calming them down. At other times in my fantasy world of Ni Noo and my father, it was my mother whom I blamed. As the war years passed by I fed on the inner belief that eventually when I grew up I could return home to Shanghai and live again. So my childhood was spent in a state of hibernation encased in an iron-clad barrier, which made Auntie and Uncle uneasy because I made no effort to make friends. I was afraid to get involved too deeply, afraid to let go, in case, like my contemporaries, I, too, married a coal-miner and became another Auntie. I did not want to endure the coal-dust, the filth and the tar smell which pervaded and seeped into our clothes. While Auntie sat alone in the front room, in one of her periodic black moods, I pounded Uncle's mining clothes with the wooden dolly and watched the water turn to a frothy grey. It seemed as grey as my life. If I had been able to put my arms around Auntie, I might have broken the emotionless existence, but I could give no affection and so received none. I ignored the licentious glances of clumsy boys who waited on street corners and shouted crude invitations. Once when I took the wireless battery to be recharged, they followed me and offered to carry it if I would let them 'have a feel'. Shame made me turn and swing the glass battery and strike the nearest boy; as I ran the acid spilt and burned great brown holes in my coat. I could not cry for sympathy but instead tried to appease Auntie by getting out the coconut shell, grinding down the carbon stick from a used torch battery and polishing the black-leaded grate until it shone. I grew up physically strong through hard work but with a spirit so weak and cowardly that I had to hide it under a veneer of sullen indifference. It was a relief to Auntie, when at the age of fifteen, two years after the war was over, my mother offered to take me back.

It was autumn 1945 when I came to live for a time in my mother's house. She had made a new life in which her children had no part because the war had made it easy by taking them away from the bombing of London. She had let off the top part of the house to Spanish exiles, students and out-of-work cabaret artists. It was a contrast to the dreary routine life of the Midlands. I had become a thin glowering girl strictly brought up in a Methodist community and suddenly found myself transported to the ups and downs of postwar London life where mother's boarders came down to her basement living room and spoke freely of their sexual adventures. Nurses wept over their lost virginity. A homosexual Spanish waiter had his bruises bathed after a fight with his boxer boy-friend. I sat silent in a corner of the living room listening to my mother advising or screaming abuse, depending on her mood. If she was not in the house when I came home from school, I automatically searched under her pillows for suicide notes informing me where I would find her body. She never realized the mental anguish she created in me, because we could never establish a mother–daughter relationship. I needed her but resented the emotional stress and instability she inflicted on me. I always looked sullen. This irritated my mother and so the antagonism grew more bitter.

A Chinese student from Shanghai rented a room in my mother's house and I asked him to advertise in a Shanghai newspaper for my father's whereabouts. It was a faint hope that he might still be alive. We also made contact through Friends House. A few weeks later my father wrote and the first of large monthly cheques arrived. Our life was suddenly transformed. My brother was removed from his unhappy foster home and placed as a boarder in a well-known public school. During holidays, he reluctantly came home, called us 'rotters' and retired unhappily to his room scraping away mournfully at his violin. 'In the deep mid-winter, frosty winds may blow', sliding the bow up and down in a slow howling protest. Our Chinese lodger basked in the atmosphere of our gratitude while he wrote letters to my father describing secretly the kind of life we lived. In his replies my father urged him to get me away from the influence of my mother. I wrote and begged him to let me come back to China. If I wondered why he never came to see us it was easily explained by his business commitments. Later I realized that he hated my mother so much that even the thought of his children was not enough to overcome the animosity. Instead, he urged me to study hard before thinking of coming back, and to get into contact with the Chinese Embassy where they would 'help and guide' me.

Our Chinese boarder introduced me to the China Institute – a club for Chinese students. It was a haven from the chaos of home and I felt the Chinese faces around me were part of my real life. For a spell I could forget my mother and all the troubled humanity of her boarding house. I did my home-work in the quiet civilized atmosphere of the club while I picked up a few words and phrases of Chinese from the languages officer of the Chinese Embassy. He was a captain in General Chennault's Flying Tigers – a war hero. To my sixteen-year-old eyes he epitomized all that I thought was good in China. He was gentle, kind and patient. He educated me from my rough Midland ways and made me feel ashamed of them and my background. It was as if I was emerging from a bad dream and this gentle officer was helping to bridge the abyss of my English life back to Shanghai, my father and civilization. The thought that in a few months he was going to be my husband was beyond my wildest dreams. I regarded myself as an ignorant inferior because my whole life in England had helped to indoctrinate me against being an equal. When I was in the Midlands the air-raid warden had come round distributing earplugs. He had given Auntie two pairs and an odd one. 'For the buzz bombs,' he had hurriedly explained. Uncle was puzzled until Auntie concluded that the odd one was mine 'because she's Chinese and not entitled'. We had all believed that this was right and proper. If the bombs fell, then I would have to stop my other ear with a piece of paper.

The Chinese students did not show their contempt in such a crude way but I sensed their patronizing attitude and accepted it. Don took me to operas and concerts and while I enjoyed the concerts because much of the music had been played at chapel, operas bored me. Afterwards he took me home, knocked on the door and handed me over to my mother, very polite and correct but always refusing her effusive invitation: 'Come in and have a cup of tea'. I was glad he never accepted because I was ashamed of the inevitable questioning and the line of washing across our living-room ceiling.

If my sullen ways irritated my mother before, my new happiness irked her even more. The hope and sense of retrieving an identity had given me new life and it showed in my face. I began to be alive and to show the contempt I felt for her and her kind. I resented her spending my father's money and the anger that had slowly smouldered finally erupted in a screaming hysterical outburst in which I left and sought shelter at the Chinese Embassy and to find Don.

We were married a few weeks later, five months after my sixteenth birthday. Don had asked my father's permission to marry me before he asked me. He had arranged for my father to telephone me from Shanghai 'with some important news concerning your future'. For the first time since I was a child of six I heard my father's voice over the crackly lines and I cried with all the pent-up loneliness, despair and longing that had been suppressed for so many years. I heard my father giving his permission for me to marry Don, but the news did not really strike me in the midst of excitement at hearing my father's voice.

'I suppose I ought to do it the English way and get on my knees to make a formal proposal of marriage,' Don said when I put the receiver down. I think then I knew it was the right thing to do, and it was as if events since I first contacted my father through the Chinese lodger had led up to that moment. I put the now-dead receiver down and walked straight into his waiting arms.

Auntie and Uncle came to the wedding and there was a brief reconciliation with my mother for form's sake. But inside me as I looked at her during the lavish Embassy reception I was determined that she would no longer be part of my life. I hated her for what I regarded as her disloyalty to my father and for her rejection of me, his daughter.

Auntie, looking at me in my wedding finery, said: 'You must wear something blue,' and took a replica of Blackpool Tower with a blue glass bead off her neck and placed it round mine. That was the nearest she had ever come to any sort of affectionate embrace and I looked at her with gratitude for the shelter and security she had provided.

I was proud of my handsome Chinese captain. I could take his scarred hands into mine and listen endlessly to his tales of air battles with Japanese fighter planes. But I was a passive partner in his love-making, there was no great passion. I could not willingly put my arms around him nor did I like him to touch me. I loved him much better in uniform. The post-war years had thrown up Frank Sinatra for girls of my age to scream and adulate while I had my own 'star'; that part of our life was a necessary sacrifice for the other advantages that being married to Don gave me – his love, his security and his Chineseness, and it was as my father wished.

We got more and more involved with left-wing students at the China Institute and were reluctant to join the social life of the Chinese Embassy. There were serious political discussions with Ph.D and others in our flat and I could see Don was becoming interested in the emerging power of the Chinese Communists still fighting a guerrilla war in the North of

China. The discussions and arguments were always in Chinese and I did not understand but as they talked and argued into the small hours, I read books on Communist China. A favourite of mine was Gunther Stein's *Challenge of Red China*. I could conceive more easily than they what a working-class revolution meant because my Midlands background, including tales of Uncle's personal experience of the General Strike, gave me a lead in a practical way while theirs was still theoretical.

Soon Don's involvement with left-wing students was relayed back to the Nationalist Government in China and he was ordered to return. We still had my father's wedding cheque and with this we decided to return with Ph.D and friends to Hongkong and from there make our way to the liberated areas of North China.

The civil war in China was intensifying. At the end of 1948 the Communists launched an offensive. Don studied the press avidly and there I felt a little uneasy at his reactions. He spoke wistfully about his friends in the air force and the happy times he spent in the Flying Tigers. He had a great love for America and I could see the internal struggle that was taking place but was not able to understand or help because I had no strong ties or family to influence me. The childish longing for my father had been, in part, replaced by Don and so the decision to go to the liberated areas seemed to me uncomplicated. On looking back, I think Don at that time would have been relieved if the Nationalists had won.

It was in the hotel in Hongkong that Don finally began wavering. We were due to leave with Ph.D and friends in a few days on a slow boat through the territorial waters still held by the Nationalists. He suggested we waited, as my father was doing in Shanghai. America was pouring military aid to bolster up the demoralized Nationalist Government and the Communist offensive had halted. I went to have a bath and as I sat washing, Don pushed open the door, pulled down his trousers and sat on the lavatory. 'Between husband and wife there should be no privacy,' he said defiantly. Embarrassed I stared at the wall in front of me, while he discussed the possibility of the Communists being defeated.

'I know best,' he said seriously, still sitting on the lavatory, but all I could think at that moment was when he was going to leave that undignified position and let me finish my bath. I could not bring myself to look at him and quickly wrapped a towel around myself and went out of the bathroom. He was no longer my handsome fighter pilot in a be-ribboned uniform. My picture had changed to an ugly little man sitting on a lavatory pan. It was easy for me to believe I was noble in wanting to make necessary sacrifices in working for a revolutionary cause. My Midlands upbringing for social justice had been the unconscious influence, so that like a new convert to Christianity I could only see the romantic image of a Communist hero. I really did not need Don any more, he was just a step in the ladder.

'I see,' I said quietly and walked out of the hotel.

Hongkong is not the best place to wander about late at night and I walked the streets for hours clutching my bag tight for fear of pickpockets. I was frightened now and did not know what to do. My student friends were in a cheap boarding house on the other side of the bay in Kowloon and I could not reach them until morning. I found a rickshawman and said in pidgin English: 'You findee me one cheap place, just for one night.' He nodded and took me to a sleazy-looking boarding house. The proprietor looked at me strangely and said something in Cantonese. I shrugged my shoulders, I did not understand. I was too tired and he showed me to my room. It was very narrow, almost like a cubicle. The walls were of carved latticed wood with paper intersected between. I could hear giggles and grunts on either side of my room but I was feeling too tired to complain. I took off my dress and lay down in my petticoat and was just dropping off to sleep when the door opened with a crash and in walked an American sailor.

'Hiya honey,' he shouted, 'You're a beaut!' and he banged the door shut with his foot and began to take off his jacket. I looked up, and then it dawned on me what I had walked into. Trying to be as dignified as possible, I pulled the sheet up to my chin and said coldly, 'Get out.' He looked at me, grinned and said: 'Holy cow. This is great!' and ripped off his shirt. Then I was hopping mad. I stood on the bed, brandished my fists and shouted in my best Midlands accent: 'Bugger off,

21

you dirty devil. I'm not a bloody prostitute!'

He stopped short and looked surprised. 'Gee whiz, 'mam, I truly am sorry. Beg yo' pardon 'mam.' He backed out and softly shut the door. I pushed the bed against it and sat there listening to the giggles, the beds creaking and the occasional door slam as each satisfied customer left on either side of the wall. I was tempted to poke a hole in the paper just to satisfy my curiosity but caution prevailed. Instead I leaned against the bedposts and laughed to myself as I wondered what Auntie and Uncle would say if I wrote and told them.

I woke up to a sudden quiet and as I lay there the dawn gradually brought in the noise of the Hongkong streets. Wooden clogs clip-clopped from a distance, getting louder till they passed by the silent sleeping hotel to fade away again in the distance. Then, as though it were a signal, the clogs heralded the dawn chorus of the back streets of Hongkong. Hundreds of clogs clattered past, voices and cries of children, the brushing of teeth, gargles and the incessant hawking and spitting which accompanied the morning ablutions.

I lay on the bed and debated what I should do. Telephone my father in Shanghai and ask him to come and get me? Or try to persuade Don? Perhaps when he saw how determined I was he would decide after all to come with me? All I could see was the picture of him sitting on the lavatory and try as I might I could not conjure up the previous image I had of him as a handsome young officer.

I pulled the bed away from the door and went downstairs. The same proprietor stood behind the desk. He grinned rather sheepishly, showing a flash of gold teeth. I looked him straight in the eye as if to dare him to laugh or make a comment and said in English: 'I want some breakfast!' He nodded and bowed me to a table in the dining room. Gradually the room began to fill up with tired young Chinese girls dressed in gaudy, satin skin-tight dresses, the slits going right up to their thighs. They stretched and yawned, delicately placing their finger-tips against an open mouth and then slumped down, their legs stretched out wide before them, vulgar and too tired to keep their legs together. A bowl of rice porridge flavoured with wafers of fish and vegetables and a poached egg nestling in the middle was placed before me. It was delicious. The others had the same. It acted as a reviver, because soon the room was full of chatter, noise and laughter. The room went silent when I got up and paid my bill, only to resume with laughter and louder chatter when I went through the door. I could not understand so it did not matter. I went to look for my student friends and then telephone my father. When the splutters died down, he ordered me to return to Don. 'He is your husband, you must do as he suggests.'

'But I don't love him,' I wailed. He said: 'Love has nothing to do with it. Look what it did to your mother and me!' He was sending me another cheque so that I should return to England with Don until the political situation had cleared up in China. He turned a deaf ear to my pleading that I should be allowed to come to Shanghai just to see him. 'Go back to your husband,' he replied. 'He is a good man from a respectable family.'

I could not tell him the truth about why we had parted. I felt a terrible sense of loss and rejection. Surely he could spare a few hours to fly down and see me? I wondered if it was because he hated my mother so much that the thought of seeing me, her daughter, was repugnant to him. I turned to my friends: 'He doesn't really want me, all he does is send money.' I made arrangements to use the money to buy a black-market ticket for a place on a cargo boat to North China.

As the boat wallowed its way through the Yellow Sea, I began to worry about what the reception would be when I arrived. Where could I go now that Don wasn't here with me? What was I going to say? Was it really true after all, what the British press had been reporting of Communist atrocities? And then I calmed my fears with the thought that if this was not the answer to my search for an identity, it would not matter any more because I would rather die than return to England.

Just two days away from the Port of Tientsin, three young men donned cloth workers' caps and red armbands and began organizing the groups of students and finding out their particulars. My friends had hidden me between the top of the hatch and a wall and told me to lie low. They were not so much afraid of the Chinese on the boat, who treated me rather like a mascot, but of the British officers who periodically came and checked the hygienic and health conditions on the over-crowded deck. Ph.D and the professor planned to take me to the organization responsible for overseas Chinese returning to their homeland. 'But we need to play it by ear,' explained Ph.D. His earnest eyes behind their rimless spectacles looked worried at the thought of the heavy responsibility I had placed upon him and the others. They had been reluctant to help me, after I had turned to them for help when I walked out on Don, but finally agreed as long as I did not involve them if there was trouble. The professor, whom the others respected as a brilliant man, was far too preoccupied with his new language machine, which simultaneously translated several languages, and trying it on me, to bother with minor problems such as getting me into Communist China. He had a captive guinea-pig in me to try to teach Chinese, Spanish, French and an obscure Tibetan dialect. He was oblivious to his surroundings and allowed the others to collect his rice and salt fish which was dumped in wooden containers twice a day at one end of the deck. We rolled out his bedding and generally acted as nurse-maid. He was very short-sighted and wore thick pebble glasses. His one and only tie was in shreds while the seat of his trousers was threadbare and had a hole. Appearance and general comfort were unimportant details compared to the mass of brilliant thoughts and theories that came out of his agile brain. When I saw him pushed and jeered at by bird-brained young wives joining their soldier husbands on the liner that carried us from England to Hongkong, all I could see were their silly flouncy cotton frocks bought with precious clothing coupons, while he probably shoved his in a drawer and forgot them. I felt humiliated for him but he was unaware of anything outside the particular concept he was working on, and left me to express my loathing by wearing beautiful brocades and silks sent me by my father and flaunting them whenever they appeared. It was a silly childish thing to do but I felt it was one step towards aligning myself with China against these representatives of all I abhorred in England. Now that the professor had a captive student on board he tried to teach me Chinese with the aid of his invention.

I depended on this returning group of Chinese intellectuals to help me through the language barrier, but they were unsure of what the reception would be once we entered Communist territory. My main concern was to get to my destination. Once I was actually on Chinese soil things would sort themselves out. I was so confident that I was God's gift to the Chinese people, with my superior English upbringing, that the thought that I might not be welcomed with open arms never occurred to me. Perhaps an older and wiser person would have hesitated before embarking on an adventure with such an ignorant assessment of oneself and of the possible outcome. But I was young, earnest and only seventeen, with already one discarded husband.

Now I stood outside Tientsin Railway Station waiting while the others went to get tickets for Peking. It was my first glimpse of the real China, cold and very dusty. There were tall buildings belonging to the foreign merchants and businessmen pitted with bullet holes from the battles which had taken place between Communist and Nationalist troops just a few weeks ago. A little beggar child sat in the dust by my feet and looked up at me with his hand held out appealingly. Flies like black scabs sucked the moisture from his eyelids and mouth. I had the remains of a tin of English biscuits under my arm with which I had supplemented the diet of rice and salt fish on the boat. I handed him one. This was immediately grabbed by a bigger child who stuffed it into her mouth before others hastened to surround me, begging with outstretched hands. I began to get hemmed in and I panicked at the scores of dirty sore-covered beggars that now began to pull at my clothes begging and whining. I emptied the rest of the biscuits on to the ground and fled. I sat on a bench in the station and tears began to stream down my face. I could not explain to my worried friends who turned up with the tickets why I was crying. There was not one specific reason but so many feelings mixed with despair, disappointment, gladness and anxiety which poured out into one great anti-climax. These beggars were my people, this poverty was the one I had exchanged for the poverty of the mining village from which I had come. I had rejected my Staffordshire coal-mining family for this. It was too late to turn back now.

Still in the middle of the group of students, we managed to get on a Peking-bound train. It was packed with garlic-smelling humanity. Pedlars walked up and down the aisles, selling things to eat. There were smoked ducks' gizzards, pickled eggs and melon seeds. Then I saw something which I remembered eating when a little girl in Shanghai seated on my father's lap as we rode home in a rickshaw.

'I'll have some of that,' I said, pointing to some grey strips of meat. A piece of newspaper curled into a cone and the pedlar put in a handful of the meat.

'Mmm,' I said to Ph.D who was looking at me with horror. 'Delicious – that brings back memories.'

'Do you know what that is?' he asked. 'It's a pig's intestines – very unhygienic. They make it in chamber pots!'

I looked at Ph.D, so prim and proper. He had enjoyed the genteel life at Oxford. Breakfast, lunch, high tea and dinner, a life that was as alien to me with my working-class English background as these greasy strips of meat and the sweat and smell of the crowded train were to him – an intellectual from a wealthy Chinese family. On the boat he had scorned the salt fish and opened up tins of sweet condensed milk to pour over his rice.

I looked at him, wondering what he would have thought of me if I had been eating chips out of a piece of newspaper instead. The difference was there, but it was not so much a difference in race but in class. Ph.D's motives in joining the Communists were patriotism and nationalism based on political theory. Mine was a mixture of romanticism and the search for an identity. My upbringing in a Midlands coal-mining community was my motivation and my memories of a Shanghai childhood the spur. Put together they led me to this train travelling to Peking and the Red Army.

Ph.D cleaned his spectacles and lectured me on the dangers of dysentery. 'Always wash water melons,' he said earnestly.

'These people,' he waved his beautifully shaped hands around him, 'are resistant to such diseases. It is a question of the survival of the fittest. Otherwise,' he frowned, 'our population would be double.' Then as a complete after-thought he said cheerfully. 'I think, on the whole, the orange is the most perfect of fruits.'

I finished off the last of the meat strips, wiped my greasy fingers on the newspaper and threw it on to the dirt-strewn floor. Dysentery, water melons, I did not care. To me those pieces of meat and the smell were the first recognizable link between my childhood and now. I looked out at the passing scene of paddy fields and the dusty yellow plains which stretched as far as the eye could see. I drew a deep breath and filled my lungs with the garlic fumes around me and licked my greasy fingers again.

When I left England to return home to China I discarded my hated English name and took back the name my father had given me: Cheo Ying. That was my real name and this was my real life. The Midlands – grey and smoky, 'Uncle' coughing his life away and 'Auntie' wondering where she had gone wrong with her ''vacuee wench' who had given up God to 'join them there Communistics' – belong to a girl once called Esther Cheo.

2
Early Days

Peking Station was crowded with people carrying huge
bundles of bedding and boxes, live chickens and ducks. A
man pushing a cart with about twenty live squealing pigs,
each individually wrapped in its own bamboo cage, separated
me from the others. I moved forward towards the barrier.
There armed guards were scrutinizing the passengers as they
went through. My heart sank, I knew that this was as far as I
was going to go. I could not shout to the others in case they
were stopped too, and as previously arranged we were to go
our own ways once we were all settled. Ph.D turned round to
see the guard's hand fall on my shoulder and pull me to one
side. He nodded and went on. I was pushed into a group
which included a German woman married to a Chinese professor returning to his old university of Ching Hua. When the
last passengers had gone through the barrier we were driven
in jeeps to a small building not far away. I guessed that the
three young men on the boat had tipped off the security
guards because they had given me some curious glances. As I
was not on their list they were unable to deal with me and had
probably passed on the information.

'Aren't you afraid?' the German woman asked, when a
little later we sat in the hot dusty office.

'Afraid of what?' I asked. I was bouncing one of her three
fretting children on my knee singing, 'Half a pound of tup-
penny rye', and then letting the child slide through my legs on
the 'Pop Goes the Weasel', and we were smiling at the
screams of excited laughter from the child.

'Of being in this strange country all alone. You poor child.'

She looked at me pityingly. I was annoyed and replied
rudely:

'Nothing is going to happen to me. At least I'm Chinese.'

I put the child down and turned my back and stared at a picture of Karl Marx. She and her husband left soon after with a crowd of smiling welcoming colleagues from his old college. She patted my head and said to her husband: 'That poor child, what will become of her?'

I sat in the office alone except for a Red Armyman seated behind a desk. Now the German woman had gone I wished I had opened my heart to her so that she could see what a frightened person I really was. The euphoria that had kept me going through the squalid crowded conditions of the boat, the train ride to Peking full of my self-importance had now left me and I wanted someone to come and treat me like a little child and protect me from this strange unknown world.

The Red Armyman fiddled with his pen, took the cap off and put it back on again, pretended to write, looked at me and quickly glanced away, then fiddled again, got up, looked out of the door and then sat down. I could feel the sobs coming up in my throat and waves of near-hysteria beginning to take over. He said something to me but I could not understand and I shook my head trying to keep the pain in my throat from rising and making me cry. He smiled but gave up and continued looking embarrassed. In the meantime my belongings were being searched. They found a music box, with a clockwork mechanism and another soldier appeared with it rather excited and pointed to it. I thought they wanted me to play it and went to wind it up. The guard snatched it away quickly and spoke fast and excitedly.

With an impatient gesture of annoyance I grabbed the box and wound it up. They waited breathlessly. A tinny version of 'Whistle While You Work' came out. There were embarrassed grins from everyone and the soldier went out again with the music box still playing. Again I sat for what seemed like hours. I watched a bluebottle flying against the paper windows up to the paper ceiling then on to the Armyman's desk. He watched it intently, while he slowly moved his cupped hand forward and with a quick swipe had it buzzing in his fist. He shook his hand and then threw the fly hard on to the floor, where it lay stunned. He brought his foot down on it, there was a small crunch and we both let out a sigh of relief.

I was feeling thirsty; the pig's intestines on the train had been very salty and I was also getting irritable. 'I want a drink,' I said, pointing to his mug on the table and then to my mouth. He immediately got up, happy to be able to do something at last, went out and reappeared seconds later with a mug of green tea. I took a gulp before I realized that it was boiling hot, and it burned my mouth. This was too much. I burst into tears.

The soldier rushed out of the room shouting at the top of his voice. Fortunately Ph.D and the Professor appeared, accompanied by another Red Army officer dressed in the shabby faded cotton uniform. He rather hesitantly asked me questions while Ph.D interpreted. When they established that my father was Chinese and was somewhere in Shanghai, the question of my nationality was no longer a problem. I was a Chinese citizen born in China. The next difficulty was what to do with me. They could not class me as an 'Overseas Chinese' because those are foreign-born. So that was not the proper organization for me. The officer was in a quandary. I could not speak Chinese, I had no qualification; it looked as if I was going to be a problem. I felt very small indeed. 'I'll do anything, anything,' I said eagerly, my self-confidence fast disappearing.

There were no civil administrations that could use my talents, such as they were. China was still immersed in a civil war. Ph.D assured me that once peace had been restored some place would be found for me. But in the meantime – the best thing was to become a recruit in the Red Army and to learn the language as soon as possible. I would join a group of other young people. The main part of our army life would involve ideological reorganization, political study and menial jobs involved in army life. Ph.D added a little of his own to the discussion. 'I don't know whether they'll be glad or sorry. Or whether you will be able to take it. It's going to be tough.'

They stayed with me until a lorry came to take them away to their destination. They had played an important part in my life and then left it when they saw me settled as they had promised they would; I was grateful. They were going for ideological reformation along with hundreds of returning

Chinese graduates from the western world. It was agreed that my ideological remoulding needed a different environment and I was joining a group of young workers and peasants to form the New Fourth Army. But for all of us there was to be no civilian life for another year and during that time we were just ordinary recruits.

A jeep arrived to take me to a small village outside the city walls of Peking. My music box was tucked under my arm but various bits and pieces were discarded on the way. I remember contemplating a smashed bottle of Dettol soaking away into the dust and saying to myself, 'I bet that's the most antiseptic piece of ground in the whole of China.' By the time I reached the other side of the city wall I had given or thrown away as unnecessary luxuries many possessions which I had thought would be useful in my new life. 'Here,' I said to the soldier fly-killer, 'a present,' and I handed him a two-foot-high pagoda made out of icing sugar from my wedding cake in London. I left him looking bewildered at these strange foreign customs.

My bedding was rolled and tied with a piece of rope which I had slung round my shoulder and anything else I could tuck inside the roll. As the jeep went through the city of Peking it set up clouds of dust, scattering the pigs, chickens and dogs that roamed the narrow lanes. All I could see were walls and I wondered where all the houses were until a gate opened inside a wall and I peeped through and saw courtyard after courtyard of one-storey buildings and ornate gardens.

I was billeted in a peasant's small courtyard just outside the city walls. My new army comrades, all girls of similar age, eyed me curiously. They had been told to help me learn my native tongue quickly but they just stood and stared at this strange newcomer. I had on a blue cotton Chinese dress which had been tailored in Hongkong to show up my English bust, and high-heeled shoes. They wore the faded khaki uniform and cloth shoes. I felt awkward and ill-dressed. But after the shock was over they helped me to make up my bed; wooden boards on two trestles.

There was a lull in the fighting and no one was sure whether the Americans were going to step up their aid again to the demoralized Nationalist troops. We had been told to

31

prepare for the push south. I had visions of shooting my way down to Shanghai and bursting into my father's house with the words, 'Daddy, this is your long-lost daughter come to liberate you!' At night lying on the hard boards I hugged myself at the thought. Don had threatened to write and tell my father about my desertion but I thought he would understand and be proud of his revolutionary daughter.

Our battalion commander, Wang T'ao, was unusually tall for a Chinese, very thin and dark – a southerner. Two deep grooves etched down from the corners of his nostrils to his mouth. A veteran of the Long March and a bout of TB, the privations of the past years showed in his thin dark frame, but when he smiled his eyes came alive shining and piercing. They were round and dark – so dark that you had to peer close to see the black pupils. He had projecting teeth and wore black leather shoes which was the only distinction in dress for officers: ordinary soldiers wore cloth shoes. His uniform was faded like the rest and on his left shoulder pocket he had the faded insignia showing him to be in the Eighth Route Army. He occupied one of the main rooms in the former American Military Headquarters where he had his desk and bed in the corner with a mosquito net tucked by the side. Over his bed was a piece of rope with his flannel and a pair of socks, neatly patched with cotton cloth, hanging out to dry.

'I'm in charge of you,' he said. 'You are to come to me if you have any problems.' He hawked and spat on the bare parquet floor and I wrinkled my nose in disgust as I realized what caused the silvery streaks all over the floor: he rubbed the gobbet of phlegm away with his foot. Yet it was no more disgusting than the gobbets of phlegm that Uncle used to spit out all around the outside lavatory which I would have to scrub and scrape each week.

My stiff cotton uniform soon became baggy and faded in the Peking sun. As soon as the first shock was over my roommates soon inundated me with questions about my background. 'Is is true English people only have one straight bone in the leg and can't bend their knees?' Because of the language problem they spoke to me slowly and babyishly, brought my food and water and all the time watched my every action. When they saw I only had one flannel, they gave me another with the gesture that one should be for my face and the other for the rest of my body. When I went to the lavatory I found eyes peeping through the cracks to see if I was made the same. I had a well-developed bust and wore a bra and they regarded that as immoral. They were flat-chested and bound down any sign of a bust with a strong piece of cotton cloth. One only showed well-developed breasts if nursing a baby and then a woman fed her baby at the theatre, on the trams or even at the many political meetings we had to attend. I became very self-conscious and began to walk about with rounded shoulders. I tried not wearing a bra but my nipples became so sore rubbing against the cotton jacket that I sought relief in wearing a bra again. Often curious soldiers stopped me in the streets and asked if I was a *Sulien Peng-yo* (a Soviet friend) wearing the uniform of the Chinese Liberation army and then I rudely answered back. I so much wanted to integrate and become part of my environment, I resented being different. Then my comrades would hurry up and apologize for my rudeness, saying: 'She's only a child, she does not understand.' They were in my age group, ordinary peasant girls but with a culture I found hard to understand after my rough Midland ways. I was often criticized for my rudeness – '*K'an bu ch'i*,' (looking down on Chinese) – and there would be heated arguments. 'How can I look down on Chinese when I was looked down on in England for being one?'

Wang T'ao suggested I adjust my attitude to suit my face and said sympathetically how unfortunate it must be to have a '*kao pi-tse*' (high nose) and foreign eyes.

The professor's painstaking coaching on the way to China began to fit in recognizable patterns. The dormant Chinese language I had spoken as a child in Shanghai and forgotten in England came alive again without my being conscious that it was taking place. It seemed that one day I was finding it difficult to express even the most simple phrase and then suddenly I was speaking and discussing in Chinese with no difficulty at all, except that my Peking dialect had traces of a Shanghai accent.

Chinese army life was harsh and basic. I never questioned

why I was there or felt I needed to be treated differently. I used to say to myself when I was cold or hungry, 'This is the revolution, I am a revolutionary,' and then felt virtuous. We had two meals a day: our first at 8 a.m. was called the wet meal, a millet porridge and salt pickle; the other meal, served at 4 p.m., was called the dry meal, either boiled sorghum mixed with red beans to make it thick and solid or steamed pyramids of golden maize bread served with a boiled vegetable to which a little oil had been added to give it body. On one special occasion, the day of the inauguration of the People's Republic of China, the rumour went round that we were going to have meat. We looked forward to the meal with eager expectation. The big cauldron finally came and with it a most appetizing smell of pork. As it was lowered to the ground we could see fat pieces of meat floating on top of the cabbage. We lined up with our bowls rather like fat Mr Bumbles in our padded uniforms. As my turn came I held out my bowl and was ladled an enormous sow's nipple complete with its ring of black hairs.

One got used to the grit and mouse droppings in the millet. A hint I remembered from a Thomas Hardy novel was not to 'chaw' until the teeth met, otherwise the grit crunched between one's teeth. When you are continually hungry you stop wasting time picking out bits of foreign matter. Once I chewed on a particularly hard piece of food in my mouth and eventually, unable to swallow it, I spat it out and found it was the remains of a big black beetle. As I heaved and vomited, my revolutionary fervour was somewhat dampened.

We were given our food, our winter and summer uniforms and two pairs of cloth shoes. Each month we had a little pocket money which just about covered our basic needs, such as a piece of soap, and for the girls, a very coarse woody paper for use as sanitary towels. I once found a piece of chicken manure embedded in mine and the mystery was not solved until I went into the countryside on land reform and saw peasants making paper and using chicken manure as one of the ingredients.

If one was very careful there might be enough money left to buy a bag of peanuts or a minute pot of Nivea cream. Every month we had to make an agonizing decision. Because we had so little fat in our diet, the Siberian-type winter dried and cracked our skins and we needed the cream to alleviate the pain. Or instead we could have one glorious splurge of fatty oily peanuts. It was a choice I was never able to resolve happily, because if I fell to the temptation of buying peanuts I knew I had to go through a month of chapping, soreness and cuts.

The army had requisitioned all the empty houses left by fleeing landlords, foreigners and foreign embassies' staffs. We were moved into a beautiful house owned by French Catholic Fathers, but all the furniture, carpets and antiques were locked away in one room. We were ordered not to use or remove any of the things for our personal use. We occupied enormous rooms with ornate ceilings and fixed wall mirrors with just our army cots – bare planks on wooden trestles – our washbasin and bundle containing rice bowl, soap and flannel. Bedbugs massed between the cracks and they were a torment to my comrades. Yet there were none in my bed. I was accused of having a secret remedy and as I was trying not to antagonize by arguing I suggested changing beds with my next door neighbour Chang Teh-fang. Two nights later we poked a knife between the cracks only to find the bugs had all moved to my old bed. 'They don't like my English blood,' I explained to my puzzled comrades. Lice were a different matter. Once while drying my shirt in the courtyard, a soldier just back from the front hung his bedding on the same line. My shirt picked up some lice and for a few days I went mad searching them out. Fleas I could tolerate because I had spent many a busy hour as a child in the Midlands hunting them in the big double bed I shared with my 'foster grandma', but lice filled me with loathing.

Round the corner from our billet Wang T'ao had his office and room where we worked, studied and ate in the big canteen. Occasionally we met in his room where he gave us a briefing on the movements of the Liberation Army as it fought and drove the Nationalists further and further South. I was detailed to colour in red chalk the areas that had been captured each day, and was told that it would help me with Chinese geography. 'Soon,' he said to me, 'we will reach Shanghai and we'll find your father.' My unit patted me on the shoulder and smiled because they knew how excited I was at the prospect of finding him.

While Chang Teh-fang and my other room-mates were given administrative work to do in the offices, I had the job of sorting out the American correspondence and other paper work left by the fleeing American advisers. The American government was still pouring arms and materials into the Nationalist Army, whose officers were so corrupt that most of the equipment found its way into Communist hands. We wore American shirts, socks, and occasionally were given five-pound tins of butter which we opened and ate by the spoonful because our bodies craved for fat. My English came in useful then because I was able to sort out equipment, foodstuffs, clothes, maps and letters. American parachutes were highly prized among the girls: we cut them up and made underwear and shirts with the nylon material.

In my unit there were six girls including myself, and several young soldiers who had been wounded during the push down to Peking. They were recuperating and waiting for posts when a civil administration was set up. Their fighting days were over and they were regarded as the cream of the revolution, the little Red Devils, the term affectionately applied to the younger members of the army. While the fighting was going on, thousands of youngsters in the liberated areas were being trained as cadres to fill the administrative posts left vacant by less politically reliable officials. Those who did not flee with the Nationalists were absorbed into the system after going through examinations and self-examinations. The incorrigibles and Kuomintang officers were sent to the *Ger Ming Ta Hsuei* (Revolutionary College) set up near the Western Hills where they attended one indoctrination meeting after another. It was voluntary and places were much sought after because outside the system there was little chance of getting a decent post or position.

I was treated as an illiterate Chinese and together with the many illiterate soldiers had to attend literacy classes. Every evening we sat huddled in a bare cold room, scratching characters in the dust with a stick, or using an old slate and tracing out characters with a wet finger. There were competitions as to who could learn the most in a day. Our first written words we learnt were geared to the slogan and jargon of those days, Communist Party, Workers and Peasants, proletariat. We learnt parrot-fashion, painstakingly memorizing them with no concrete guides except memory and will-power. In three months we had learnt enough Chinese characters to be able to read the highly politically slanted army paper the *Liberation Daily*. What joy as we haltingly read out the headlines of different towns and areas being 'liberated'. It made us feel as if we were at last 'taking off our illiterate hat'. To read a simple story was still beyond our capability but all our required reading in those days consisted of political slogans and clichés because that was all we talked about. Our teacher, the wife of an army general, was responsible for wiping out illiteracy in our battalion. She wore great round spectacles far too big for her tiny earnest face and she thundered and bawled at us, dinning the characters into us until the sweat ran down our faces in the enforced concentration which gave us no lever to grasp or build upon. We were so harassed and frustrated that one burly soldier rammed his fist through the paper window one evening and ran swearing from the room: '*Ch'ao ni de ma* . . .' (f – – – your mother's . . .). She did not even pause in her tirade against our laziness. 'It is your duty as future responsible cadres to learn. . . .' When I staggered into my bed groaning with the weight of memorizing, I dreamed of Chinese characters and woke in the morning still muttering the number of characters we had to memorize by evening. When we went to our next class we found our swearing soldier colleague sheepishly writing out a self-criticism with our teacher's help. . . . 'Why did you not have a padded coat before liberation?' He muttered. 'Because I didn't have the money.' 'Yes, but why didn't you have the money? You worked hard enough?' She persisted in forcing him to think out a pattern of ideas and concepts that could be fitted with the characters he had already learned until the tears streamed down his face as he laboriously wrote out his self-criticism on a piece of paper with a pen she had lent him.

After three months our teacher decided we had learnt enough Chinese characters to be able to make simple notes of our political meetings and to read simple political essays. She congratulated us on our hard work and 'political fervour'.

'This proves you are good revolutionaries,' she said. As a celebration present Wang T'ao gave me a pen and a notebook.

There was no shortage of men for military service, while the
women in our organization were mainly concerned in paper-
work, in the medical and photographic sections, or took
charge of study groups. Sometimes a group of young girls who
resented the male chauvinism of only men being allowed to do
military training competed with them on obstacle courses and
beat them hollow, while I became a crack shot with an American rifle. The usefulness of that only came years later on an
English fairground. I did once try to shoot a pheasant for the
pot with a soldier's revolver and missed each time as the bird
slowly wended its way down the lane completely unconcerned. Wang T'ao, watching from his window, sent for me
and said: 'Do not waste bullets, they are for the enemy only.'

The afternoons and after our four o'clock meal we spent in
innumerable meetings and self-examinations, always searching for motives and reasons in everything we did or thought.
We all, at different times, took the opportunity of venting our
spite on someone we did not like, under the guise of constructive criticism. But we were soon cured of that; others always
saw through what was malice and what was genuine concern.
We were not astute enough to colour our personal dislikes
with political clichés and quotations from the works of Lenin
and Marx. It rebounded upon us and we found ourselves very
much on the defensive. Our commander, Wang T'ao, sometimes sat in on our meetings, adding very little to general
discussions, but making a note now and then in his book. Our
meetings were mainly within our own unit discussing and
analyzing our faults and listening to what others thought of
our behaviour and attitude. Occasionally we joined hundreds
of others and sat in the grounds of the main building while we
heard an important report relayed to us by Wang T'ao. Sometimes we were herded into lorries and taken to a mass meeting
with hundreds of other army personnel to hear a report by
Mao Tse-tung or the commander-in-chief, Chu Teh. Once, as
we all sat listening, during one hot drowsy afternoon, the
speaker suddenly raised his voice and the audience raised
their left hands and repeated a set of slogans. I was falling
asleep in that hot sun but raised my fist and repeated the

same words. It was a mass recruitment for the Young Communist League, and one of the last, because afterwards individuals had to prove their revolutionary fervour before they could join. I found the afternoon and evening studies of political theory irksome and hard to understand. So did the others, but for different reasons. They were trying to read badly translated Chinese from Russian which in turn had been translated from English or German. By the time it had been translated into Chinese it was so obscure that I often wondered whether the Chinese ever really studied Marxism or only some bastard version of Marxism. I managed to get English copies of the same texts and tried to explain some of the obscurities to my comrades, many of whom were barely literate, in simple graphic terms. My explanation of what I thought dialectical materialism meant went like this: 'Well, you see that rock? It doesn't stay like that forever. As each moment passes, that rock is changing into something else.'

'Changing into what?'

'I don't know that part, perhaps a scientist could tell us. But this book is trying to explain that things are never the same, they are changing all the time. It is not the same today, as it was yesterday. That's dialectical materialism.'

None of us was really capable of understanding the higher reaches of Marxism—Leninism. Mao Tse-tung with his little homely analogies helped millions to understand far more than they would ever have done in years of concentrated study. There were repercussions in later years when the intelligentsia came to the fore and for a time twisted Marxism into middle-class values and professional elitism until the rumblings erupted into the Cultural Revolution when to be an intellectual was no longer fashionable nor advantageous.

3
Pet

We saw little of Peking in those early revolutionary days, except for our immediate surroundings. The bazaar was off limits because of the danger of assassination. We had no money to go on the tram and see the sights. There were still spasmodic shootings and murders, especially of those in uniform. Beggars were still much in evidence and once I saw a man standing with his head bent down in shame, in the middle of a chalked circle. He had been caught smoking opium.

There were a lot of noughts on the currency. People's wages were worked out monthly by the cost of staple foods. Therefore, a tram-driver was paid the equivalent of some cattys of rice per month. With a stroke all the noughts were cancelled out one day, and we were back in yuans of ones and tens. It seemed a novel way of solving inflation.

Sometimes in the evenings when we were too hot to sleep or on the rare occasions when we all decided to '*san bu*' – take a stroll – we would call out to the men across the courtyard; two or three of them grabbed a pistol or rifle and followed behind us. They were the most gentle and pleasant of escorts. Sometimes on the busy main streets, they walked beside us and we chatted and joked. In the dark lanes they silently walked behind us with just the sound of their cloth shoes and the flapping of their guns in their wooden holsters echoing down the lane. They saw us to our room, and returned to their own quarters and their interrupted game of chess or books. There were still too many silent knifings from runaway dispossessed landlords who fled into the city from the surrounding countryside.

Underground secret societies, always the enemy of the

Chinese Communists, still tried to exist by trading on the fears and superstitions of ordinary people for their survival. Each criminal gang had its own complex organization. I met one scoundrel who was a wizard at mending broken bones and treating injuries sustained by burglars and robbers in their profession. Instead of being punished he was given a clinic and became a respectable manipulator of broken bones with the position of consultant to a big teaching hospital. This was one subtle way of breaking up the gangs. The worship of gods – and most beloved of all the many gods was the kitchen god, as food is so close to the heart of a Chinese – was not overtly banned but in the general uneasy atmosphere where rumour was rife in those early days, it was better not to flaunt them. Everyone felt some kind of guilt.

One of my colleagues invited me to her parents' home for a meal. She went into the kitchen and screamed at her mother for displaying a kitchen god in front of me, a fellow comrade. She felt she had lost face through her backward-thinking parents and threw the clay god into a pile of kitchen rubbish. It was a jolly-looking god and I was glad to see her mother hurriedly pick it up, wipe it clean and hide it in a stone jar of rice. We had a splendid meal cooked by my colleague's mother and I silently thanked the kitchen god.

The majority of Peking people were puzzled by the apparent friendliness of the army – the first ever army not to pillage and loot. But one could sense there was still a wary attitude adopted towards anyone in uniform. People took care not to overstep certain undefined lines, even though no new laws had yet been introduced because the government of the People's Republic of China had not been formed. We were still living in a revolutionary situation. For example, I saw an opium smoker dealt with quickly and summarily by an ordinary soldier who had caught him smoking. He had simply dealt with an unpopular social ill by making it an object of contempt and humiliation.

Religion was never a very strong point with the materialistic Chinese and was treated as just another form of superstition and lumped together with other myths and wizardry. There were some good documentary films made at that time which exposed the secrets which lay behind the magic and mystery which held people. By isolating some people, like the thieves' bone-mender who was given his own clinic, or the specially trained acrobats who could climb inaccessible places and steal who were put into State theatre groups, people with a useful potential were neutralized on the one hand and given a new purpose on the other. Criminal elements who had no useful skill to offer were rejected and became dangerous antagonists to any member of the Communist Army. So did dispossessed landlords who had fled into the cities away from revenge-seeking peasants. Remnant Kuomintang officers who had been turned down by the army and former members of Chiang Kai-shek's secret police represented another danger of personal violence. Stripped of any organizational power they still lurked in the '*hutungs*' (lanes) and bazaars waiting. If there had been any organized counter-revolutionary movement on a large-scale this had already been dealt with – long before the the main body of Communist forces had moved into the cities – by secret Communist agents and informers who had infiltrated many of these bodies and had been slowly building up dossiers, so that when the cities were liberated it was just a question of rounding them up. I was greatly surprised to find that one of our top-ranking officers, a close colleague of Wang T'ao, had been an underground agent in the Kuomintang air force and a close friend of my husband Don when they were in General Chennault's Flying Tigers Squadron during the war. He knew everything there was to know about Don's activities as a fighter pilot, even to the number of planes he had shot down, as well as complete dossiers on the flying officers of the Kuomintang air force.

In the dark winter months, it was decided that for the time being no one was allowed out of the compound because there had been some spasmodic knifings and attacks on small groups of Armymen. We were confined to our quarters. It was all the more irksome because we had discovered the delights of ice-skating on the Pei Hai lake. We had found some old-fashioned screw-on skates in one of the foreign mission houses that had been commandeered for army use. The house we had moved to was a very grand building. There was an enormous conservatory with a beautifully tiled floor, much too cold to live or sleep in. The men lodged in the east, west and north wings of the squared court-yards while the women slept in the south wings. We were bothered by a plague of stoats, yellow evil-looking animals that scampered and squeaked behind a mud partition which seemed to lead to nowhere. We asked Wang T'ao's permission to knock the wall down and destroy the stoats. It was only made of mud and straw and soon we had the job done. We found hidden behind the wall several bottles of foreign wine labelled in French. I could barely make out what the lettering said. They were mis-shapen dark dirty-looking bottles with a wax-like substance covering the cork. Yang Ming, our squad leader, knocked the top off and smelt it.

'What is it, Cheo Ying?' he asked passing me the bottle. It had a faint smell of raisins. He poured a little into his cupped hand and licked it, then spat it out with an oath: 'Terrible stuff these foreigners drink!' and flung the bottle on to the pile of mud and straw where it slowly glugged and mixed in with the dust. I took the other bottles and put them under my bed. 'I like the taste,' I said. 'I'll drink it'.

That week-end Chang Teh-fang and I drank our way through a couple of bottles to make up for our disappointment at not being allowed to skate. As we slowly became more daring in our drunken state, we decided to have our own skating rink. We opened wide all the windows of the great glassed-in conservatory and then threw bucket after bucket of water on to the tiled floor where it froze almost on impact. We had an uproarious time, screaming with hysterical laughter as we found it was much more fun to skate when drunk. In the midst of our frolics Wang T'ao appeared, summoned by an angry Yang Ming whom we had tried to drag on to our improvised ice-rink only to fall in an undignified tangle on the ground.

Our rather pathetic attempts at self-criticism the next morning were worsened by the sorry state we found ourselves in. We felt sick and ill. I had never been drunk before. In the midst of waves of nausea which kept coming over me, I heard Yang Ming criticize himself for allowing me to keep the bottles when he should have realized that old foreign wine must have gone off after such a long time. 'It must have been over a hundred years old!' he exclaimed. In between the giddy spasms I could hear Wang T'ao somehow linking up poisoned wine with the poisons of western civilization. Cheng Teh-fang offered to clean out the lats as a redemption because we could think of nothing else that could make us feel more sick and nauseous. We felt we needed scourging ourselves. Wang T'ao came and watched me smash the rest of the bottles of Napoleon brandy and throw it away.

Among the common sights in the lanes of Peking in those days were the pigs which belonged to different households. They scavenged around, never straying too far from the homes of their owners, who now and then appeared at the gate and gave a shout and their particular pig would rush at top speed with ear-splitting squeals to receive a scrap. Then back to the public lavatories in each lane. These lavatories were neat oblong holes dug in the ground with cement foot rests. What did not go down the hole the pigs cleared up. Children running about the lanes with their split trousers would have a pig waiting almost as quickly as they squatted. The pigs sensed when a child was ready to go. It seemed to be an important part of a Chinese pig's diet.

One of the jobs we had to take turns in doing was to clean out the army latrines, huge communal affairs, one great pit for the women and another for the men. When it came to my turn I was given a large wooden, tapered bucket with two large handles which you slipped over your shoulders to allow the bucket to rest on your back, and a long-handled ladle. I had to scoop out the night soil and fling it into the bucket on my back. It is an art that needs practice and for the first few days the turds flew everywhere but in the bucket. I threw it over my head, over my back, yards behind me, hitting other people if they were in the way. It became a joke. To great hoots of laughter, one young Armyman walked in front of me, banging a gong to warn people to keep away shouting: 'Take cover! Cheo Ying is coming with her flying shit machine!' Gradually I became expert and with a deft flick of the wrist was able to aim straight and ladle the stuff into the bucket on my back.

In the summer it was particularly nasty because with the heat, the lats soon filled up with a stinking mess. The flies started breeding and one scooped up ladles of writhing maggots. The smell was dreadful, especially if there had been an attack of diarrhoea or dysentery in the camp. I was criticized at one meeting because I tried to get out of my turn on one very bad day. My stomach was heaving and my clothes reeked. I was told: 'You only have to do it as part of your training, but some people do it for a living. What a bad attitude you have towards these working people.'

'I don't have to *like* doing the job,' I shouted as I went to find the bucket and scoop.

Along these huge pits were laid two planks so that several could squat along the planks. We used to call it our '*wen hua bu*' (cultural club) because none of us liked going there alone especially at night, in case we fell in. So the cry went up: anyone want to go to the cultural club? Gradually grooves were worn where hundreds of feet had rested and where one could tuck one's feet in without fear of toppling over. One day I happened to be alone in a contemplative mood when my prize possession, my Parker 51 fountain pen, fell into the pit below. I let out a howl of anguish and tottered out crying. One of the men rushed up and asked what was the matter. I pointed to the latrine and moaned: 'My Parker 51.' He sized up the situation in a twinkling and asked me to show him where I had been squatting. He bent down, rolled up his sleeve and flung his arm deep into the pit and fished around until he came up with my pen. He wiped it carefully on a piece of paper and said: 'Here you are, comrade, all is well!' I always thought afterwards what a classic example of comradeship but not one you could relate in genteel company.

Peking winters are very cold. As people squatted they huddled close for extra warmth. The faeces fell closely grouped and froze immediately on impact. Instead of spreading evenly along the pits they rose like stalagmites. When it reached a certain point, piercing the planks of wood, or in army terms threatening our rear, the column had to be hacked down like a tree. As I once watched the chips fly I could not resist a cry of, 'Timber' as the long frozen trunk of excreta crashed to the ground.

Nothing is thrown away in China and the night-soil was a valuable fertilizer. We poured the contents of our buckets into a wooden cart drawn by a donkey. Our particular donkey had one foreleg shorter than the other and it was cleverly built up with a piece of metal. The leaking cart trundled through the streets of Peking to the peasant households outside the city walls where it was spread out on the ground to dry in the sun. Then a heavy roller crushed it into a fine powder. This was shovelled up into heaps ready to be taken to the fields.

A few years later the newly formed Ministry of Health tried to encourage modern sanitation. There was a terrible outcry at the waste of such good fertilizer and the municipal night-soil collectors actually threatened to strike.

It was about this time that I decided I would never eat pork again. Rather than give the real reason and be criticized for being finicky or looking down on Chinese pigs, I said it was against my religion. Respect for people's beliefs was strongly impressed on us during our meetings so nobody dared question my 'faith', because in the pre-government days, there was a need for the Communist Party to have a broad-based united front of all religions and political parties. The reason for the sudden conversion was that I had been squatting in the loo deep in thought when suddenly I heard a grunt and at the same time something wet and cold pushed against my backside. I went flying down into the lat. Fortunately there was not much there, and when I looked round there was a big fat sow who could not wait but had crept up behind me and snouted me up the backside in order to get the last little bit. I realized why the loo had been so clean that day.

Soon pigs disappeared from the Peking scene. Peking was, after all, the capital of China, and unhygienic scenes like roaming pigs and homeless dogs were incompatible with the new image of a modern capital city.

There were thousands of homeless dogs in Peking. They wandered the streets, lanes and garbage dumps in packs, fighting with each other and with the pigs for any food scraps and excrement. They were diseased and mangy, in a pitiful condition. One day as I passed a sweet potato stall, I noticed one half-starved puppy eating the peel that customers were stripping off their hot sweet potatoes. It was not a pretty dog, its fur was matted, one ear looked as if it had been chewed off, but I watched in admiration as it deftly caught the potato peel in mid-air and lifted its lip as if grinning and waited for the skin to cool. That was one puppy I decided was not going to have the same starving existence as the others. I scooped it up in my arms where it struggled and snarled and took it back to my dormitory. I called her Hsiao Mee, named after the millet we ate, and I shared all my food with her. When I see my fat pampered dog now, I often see Hsiao Mee, making sure I shared any little luxury titbits with her, otherwise she went into tremendous sulks. We grew inseparable. It was comforting to share with Hsiao Mee the sadness I felt at times. There was no need for words as she rested her head on my lap while I sat on a step and thought of the Christmasses I had spent with Auntie and Uncle. She grew beautiful and sleek because she was the recipient of all my suppressed love, longings and sadness and a good part of my meagre rations. At night she slept at the end of my bed, keeping my feet warm in the winter and making me so hot in the summer that I would kick her off only to find her in the morning sitting up asleep in a begging position with her front paws resting on my feet.

Some of my room mates objected to a dog sharing our sleeping quarters but she harmed no one and learned whom to avoid.

I had Hsiao Mee for nearly two years when, in 1951, without warning, there was a swoop on all wild dogs. Policemen armed with wire nooses strung through bamboo poles rounded them up and took them away. Dog owners thought they were safe. But two weeks after the dogs were cleared from streets, the police broke into houses and took away the household pets. I shut Hsiao Mee in, knowing the police would not enter an official organization. But one of the girls who disliked dogs opened the door and let her out; she was caught as she ran towards the main building where I was working. Dog owners coming back to their homes found their doors had been broken down and the dogs taken. No one knew where. In desperation I went to Wang T'ao and in tears begged him to help me to find Hsiao Mee. He was embarrassed at such an emotional display over a street dog, but eventually got on the telephone and found out where all the dogs had been taken. It was miles away at the other end of the city wall. I borrowed a bicycle and found my way to an enormous compound where there were hundreds of dogs, some in cages, some small ones staggering around dying on their feet from starvation and disease. They were not fed but were either attacking and eating the weaker ones or starving to death. At this time the dogs who had been taken from people's homes were in separate cages labelled with the district they came from. I walked up and down stumbling over dead and dying dogs, shouting out Hsiao Mee's name, trying to drown out the barks and whines of hundreds of dogs. Eventually I found her. She was in a cage with several others. She jumped up and tried to lick my face, trembling with fear and perhaps excited, hoping that I had come to take her home. I could only sit there and stroke her. She licked the tears from my face, whining. I did not know how long I sat there stroking her. But even while I was there I saw one policeman put a wire noose over a pretty black and white collie-type dog and swing it round his head until it choked to death. Then he flung it down on the ground and skinned it, putting the hide still steaming from the body heat over a cage to dry with other dogs cowering underneath. He shouted across to another policeman: 'That's another winter cover for a car bonnet!' There was no anti-freeze available in Peking in those days. He flung the bloody remains into another cage whose inmates rushed forward to eat what was left.

I cycled up each day to feed Hsiao Mee, hoping that the order would come for her release. But the days went by. On one of the visits I took a pair of scissors and chopped her beautiful coat into ugly bare patches, just in case her coat was too much of a temptation. Each day I saw more dogs slaughtered, more bones and skulls bleaching in that stinking dog's Belsen. I could not sleep. I cried all night as I thought of Hsiao Mee's reproachful eyes as I left her each day. The girl responsible for letting her out to be caught moved out of our room because no one would speak to her. Eventually Wang T'ao took me in his jeep on my daily trip to try to alleviate some of her suffering. The policemen were not so callous when he was there, gave Hsiao Mee a cage to herself and promised they would treat her well. Yet despite Wang T'ao's position, there was nothing he could do to get her back. On the last day he told me the official order had been given that there were to be no dogs in Peking. He went with me again and stood there while I sat and stroked my dog. I had managed to get some scraps of pork from the canteen and as Hsiao Mee, grotesque in her chopped-up coat, shivered and ate from the bowl, I held out my hand for Wang T'ao's pistol. He took the safety catch off. I pressed the barrel against her ear and blew her head off.

4
Father

In the summer of 1949 Shanghai was liberated. The Communist People's Army took over the city peacefully without a shot being fired. A committee of local Chinese dignitaries signed the peaceful surrender of Shanghai.

Wang T'ao never mentioned my father and I was too shy to remind him of his promise that he would find him when Shanghai was liberated.

The meetings and study period were over and we were eating our final meal of the day. It was sorghum, a kind of purple barley boiled with red beans which gave the rather tasteless grain a meaty taste. I preferred this to millet because it was less stony. The vegetable was boiled turnip flavoured with soya sauce and a handful of dried shrimps. To give the dish more body some cotton seed oil had been added. The oil floated on top encircling each tiny insect with its own halo of gold. We ate in the No. 3 canteen (*Ta Tsao*), the mess which catered for the mass of ordinary soldiers, officials and technicians. No. 1 canteen (*Hsiao tsao*), called the small mess, was reserved for party leaders and generals such as Mao Tse-tung and Wang T'ao. They had a meat dish with polished rice and steamed bread made from white wheat flour.

I was cleaning out my bowl and chopsticks when Wang T'ao sent down his bodyguard to say he wanted to see me. As I raced up the stairs I hardly dared hope that it might be news of my father. I began to think of what 'crimes' I might have committed that deserved a rocket. As soon as I entered his room and saw his smiling face I knew he had good news.

'You've found him! You've found him!' I shouted and flung my arms round his neck with sheer happiness. He put his arms around me and rubbed his hairless cheek against mine.

Wang T'ao had a letter written by my father which also enclosed a letter to a former school-mate of his who was a member of the Central Committee of the Chinese Communist Party. In great florid writing reminiscent of the old style my father reminded him of their school days together and asked him to look after his beloved daughter who was now a member of the People's Liberation Army. Wang T'ao and I looked at each other and I pulled a face. 'I don't think we need to send this on, do you?' I shook my head. He tore it up and threw the letter into the spittoon.

We read my father's letter which told me all about my Chinese brothers and sisters, and details about his family which he had kept from us before. He made no mention of mother. His omission was masterly in its studied indifference. I looked forward to the day when I could get leave to visit my new found family.

By an ironic twist of fate, my father was arrested several weeks later on charges of bribery and corruption. He had done what was normal during the Japanese occupation and under the Nationalists, when bribes oiled many wheels. But he found it a different matter when he tried to bribe the new Communist officials in order to get contracts. A charge of spying for the Americans was added. He had tried to establish trading relations with his associates in the United States, thinking the Communists would jump at the chance of having links with the Americans. He was sadly mistaken. If he had tried twenty-five years later he might have been treated more favourably, but in those early anti-American days his attempts were interpreted as 'spying'. Whatever the detailed charges were, they could not have been so very serious because he was given a relatively light sentence by the standards of those times; eight years 'labour reform'. He was transported to the bleak North-West to build roads.

'I shall never see him now,' I said in despair to Wang T'ao. He gave me a comforting hug and I could feel the heat of his body through his thin cotton uniform. 'It will be kill or cure for him,' he said. The North-West was not a very hospitable place, a bleak sparsely populated wilderness which the Chinese were developing as an isolated area to stockpile and establish military and eventually nuclear weapons. Wang

T'ao found his address and for several years we corresponded. At first the letters were full of self-pity, complaining of the bad food, which seemed no worse than what I was eating, the cold and the endless self-examination meetings. He had to 'work like a coolie, and as you know my dear daughter, your daddy has never been in good health. My specialist in the States had advised against strenuous exercise.' He begged me to use my influence to get him off heavy work and transferred to a white-collar job. 'After all,' he argued, 'I can't be as bad as these opium addicts and thieves who are my companions now.' He still could not accept that there was nothing I, nor anyone else, could do. It was not the old days any longer when a little bribery could smooth a troubled path. Gradually his letters became more resigned and even cheerful. He described a mountain that he had to climb carrying loads of rocks. It was similar to one his family had owned in Szechuan Province. He used to be carried up in a sedan chair by sweating coolies, so that he could sit in a little pagoda on the top, savour the cool breeze, admire the view, sip tea and compose some lines of poetry. 'Now,' he wrote, 'I can run up and down it like a jack rabbit. I have never felt so well in all my life.'

As his mood changed so did his work. The authorities discovered that he had some experience in civil engineering. In his student days in London when he was full of political idealism, he had studied for a time in the John Laing engineering company. 'At last I am fulfilling the dream of my youth. Why wasn't I born twenty years later?'

All his property had been confiscated after his sentence. His wife and children were left with nothing. My stepmother, whom my father had married for her youth and beauty, was ill-equipped for earning a living. But as she could read and write English she was given a job as a teacher. She still found it difficult to make ends meet with five children. My father begged me to remember my duty as the eldest of the family to help support my young half-sister and half-brothers. Wang T'ao also reminded me of my duty as the eldest child, and to my surprise I discovered it was not uncommon for high-ranking officials to support family dependents because their rich peasant landlord heads of families were serving sentences for various misdemeanours. A strange mixture of rough justice and humanity.

I had to remain on the supply system for a number of years and forfeit any future salary I would be entitled to while getting just my food and clothes free and the small amount of pocket money. What I did not have I would not miss and so each month a money order was sent by the army to my Chinese dependents. Each month the children dutifully wrote a letter of thanks and gave a report on their progress at school. I, in turn, wrote back encouraging letters of support. Wang T'ao couched my letters in a style suitable for a person who had suddenly assumed the status of head of such a large family.

This arrangement continued for well over eight years as there is no remission of sentence in China. My father's eight years went up to nearly ten years before he was finally released. He was doing a useful job in the North-West and the authorities were reluctant to let him go. When finally his release papers came through he was offered the same position with a salary. To my disappointment he turned it down. He was eager to get back to the civilization of Shanghai. He wrote: 'Beer is three times the price here as it is in Shanghai. The cost of living is too high.' He threw away an opportunity that he would have felt an honour to accept had he been a young student when the same position was offered him. The North-West was the golden land of promise for so many young Chinese men and women who were willing to sacrifice material wealth for the rigours of opening up new land. My father seemed to have learnt nothing. The rot and corruption of Shanghai had been too ingrained for any qualitative change. In the meantime, the two eldest children had finished college, a girl as a doctor and a boy in mathematics. They became part of a huge volunteer force of graduates who moved to the North-West — the place my father rejected. When he returned to Shanghai it had changed so much from when he had first left it ten years before to serve his sentence, I wondered if he had any regrets. By then I had lost the need for a family. The organization was my home, my parents and my security. When my father wrote to say he would call and see me on his way back from his exile, I sent him one last letter not to bother. 'We have no need for each other any more. Go back to your own family.'

I warned my comrades that if he should come to the office compound asking for me, to say I had gone away. I was not sure that the slender memories I had built my life upon, enlarged so that they had governed my whole behaviour as a child, might prove too much of a let-down if I saw him now stripped of all the grandeur I had built around his memory and asking for my pity. I could not trust myself not to hate him and I asked my group to help me decide. I wanted to push the decision on to someone else so that I could have a guiltless conscience.

'Do not see him. What is past can never be the same,' advised Huang Chen. I felt relief that he had decided for me.

One evening as I was entering the gate, I saw Hsiang Li, a young man whom I called my big brother, edging out a middle-aged weatherbeaten man past me. I heard him say: 'No, she left last week. I don't know where she has gone'.

'Who was that?' I asked when he came back.

'Nobody special.'

Later in the evening, I looked up from my book and said: 'That man was my father, wasn't he?'

'Yes,' Hsiang Li said.

'I thought so,' and I continued reading.

I never saw him.

He died when I was six years old and the memory of my father as he was then, clever, kind and loving, remains untarnished.

5

Land Reform

The rains had come and gone, emulsifying the Peking dirt and dust into an even finer powder. Bicycles set up clouds of dust as they went by. Many of us took to wearing white surgical masks to keep out the dust that irritated our throats and noses but the stillness of the air and the humidity made it difficult to breathe. Our eye lashes collected little droplets of moisture from the damp air we breathed out through our masks which in turn attracted dust particles and clogged up the corners of our eyes. Peking has a harsh climate.

Towards the end of 1949 most of China was in Communist hands and the turning over of land to the millions of peasants was well under way. Groups of cadres were sent out to the villages to observe and to take part in land reform. We had been on various preliminary day visits and studied the problems we would encounter and how to tackle them when our turn came. The discussions meant little to me as I was not a landowner but to my colleagues, many of whom came from peasant or small land-owning backgrounds, the right approach and attitude towards dividing up land fairly among the landless and land-hungry peasants were very important. I could understand why my friend Chang Teh-fang, commonly known as '*Pang Tse*' (Fatty) became so heated when she said: 'We are not wealthy landlords. My father had to scrimp and scrape to scratch a living from his land, as did his father and grandfather before him. What we've got we've had to work for.' But I also felt sympathy for Liu Jui whose parents were poor peasants with no land at all who remarked: 'So did my parents scrimp and scrape, as did their parents before them. Does it mean it is all a matter of luck if at the end of it all one family has land and the other does not? I think that land should not depend on luck but on equality and fairness.'

I thought Pang Tse and Liu Jui had a point and it was difficult for me to judge who was more right. Pang Tse was in the minority, therefore she was wrong. Liu Jui represented the majority.

In the late Autumn of 1949, we were told to pack our things and get ready to go. Our destination was a village about twenty-five miles north of Peking called Huang T'u Hsiang – Yellow Earth Village. It was a dried-up place; the area's main produce was sorghum, which grows over six feet high with purple tassels of grain, and yellow millet that blended so well into the dried-up land from which the village took its name. The peasants' homes were in a sorry state. The recent rains had washed away great patches of mud used for the walls of their homes, exposing the frame of sorghum stalks. We were billeted in individual peasants' homes wherever possible and were expected to do our share of their work. Some of the men from the group slept in an old tumble-down temple while I teamed up with 'Fatty'. She had been at Ching Hua University until she slipped out from the campus one night just before the Kuomintang secret police started rounding up students with 'wrong thoughts'. We were billeted with Old Liu and his wife. She was a wrinkled, nearly bald, old lady with tiny bound feet which did not stop her from keeping up with the fastest walkers. We hardly heard a complete sentence from her. She was dominated by her husband who finished each sentence she started. She had got so accustomed to the habit that whenever she started to talk, she stopped half-way and waited; the long pauses were so nerve-racking that in the end we also unceremoniously finished off what she was going to say. Old Liu stood on no formality with us but was brusque almost the the point of rudeness.

'Well, it seems to be the fashion, but what two snippets like you are supposed to do I don't know.' He called me '*er mao-tse*' (Two Hat – meaning a person of mixed parentage) and poor Chang Teh-fang knew that inevitably he would use her uncomplimentary nickname, *Pang Tse* (Fatty).

He smoked the popular long-handled pipe with a leather pouch hanging from its stem and when he was not using it he stuck it down into the top of his black baggy quilted trousers which were wrapped around him and tied with a band of dirty white cloth. Sometimes if it was a warm day, he squatted outside against the wall with a couple of his cronies, squatting with ease familiar from the Midland coal-miners I used to know. Old Liu would put his pipe behind his ear and search the top of his trousers for lice, cracking them between two brown deeply ridged thumb nails. Then he would take his pipe and use it to have a long satisfying scratch at the inaccessible places.

We went out with him as soon as we unrolled our bedding in the corner of his cottage, making sure there were no cracks for scorpions to come out and hide between our clothes. I was able to smell their musty odour although my friends insisted they did not smell. Often there was a cry of '*Shie Tse Shie Tse*' and we rushed to the scene and dared each other to grab the frightened scurrying scorpion by its hooked tail and kill it. The secret was to pinch tight between finger and thumb the poisonous tip before it could strike. Old Liu took us to see some miserable-looking paddy fields which were dried up with a few broken stalks standing here and there drunkenly between the cracks. 'This field used to belong to my brother until that son of a turtle Old Kuang took it for unpaid taxes.'

He took his pipe out of his mouth and spat a stream of brown liquid.

'My brother is dead now so you can tell everybody that I want this piece of land and the bit near the well.' He went on to enlarge on the choice pieces of land he wanted. When we pointed out that all land had to be shared equally and fairly, he said, 'But you said we are all free now, we are our own master. Well, I want that land.'

It was obvious that freedom to Old Liu meant the freedom landlords had in the past. He knew no other meaning for such an abstract term.

During the day we worked hard digging irrigation ditches, and held meetings with groups of peasants in the evenings. The main landlord who had fled from the village and gone into hiding in Peking had been brought back and was imprisoned in his house waiting for the trial or 'struggle meeting'. Most of the peasants were not like Old Liu, who if he had been given the opportunity would have been an even bigger

despot than Kuang. Although we contributed more than our
share of grain and food to the household Old Liu begrudged
every mouthful we took and glared if there was too big a
helping of vegetable between our chopsticks. Yet there was a
certain fairness in his meanness. He practically counted out
the spoonful of grain each person had, including his own and
his wife's. We were perpetually hungry but to have complained would have brought a storm of criticism down on our
head. To make matters worse we had been cutting down the
dried-up maize and sorghum stalks from the temporarily
ownerless fields. The long leaves were like razors and they
had covered my bare arms with hundreds of tiny cuts. I had
not brought my cream with me in case I was thought soft by
the peasants and so some of the cuts did not heal but became
great gaping wounds. My body had not yet managed to make
up for the various deficiencies in my diet. One night I sat in
the corner of the room and cried with pain. Old Liu came in
and asked: 'What is the matter, Er Mao-tse?' I just stretched
out my arms to show him.

'Ah, that is very bitter,' he said softly. At the unexpected
sympathy I howled. He took down a bottle containing a
greyish-looking liquid. It was sesame oil in which he had
placed scorpions that he caught from time to time. The oil
was used as a peasant remedy against scorpion stings. 'I'm
not wasting good cooking oil on you, little sister, this will do
just as well.' It smelt like rotting cabbage but the oil brought
relief.

Kuang, the local despot, was finally brought to be 'struggled against' by the peasants. He looked a kindly old man,
tall, well-built and well-fed. I was curious to see what crimes
he had committed against these peasants, many of whom
were his distant relatives but who spat and swore every time
his name was mentioned. Now he stood before hundreds of
peasants with his head hanging down, not daring to look up.

It was difficult to get individuals to come up and speak
against him. He managed to instil fear even though he stood
there humbled. One woman plucked up courage to start to
say something but he glared at her with such malevolence
that the words died away and she sat down hurriedly. Gradually people got up, and at first there were timid requests that

he return grain and possessions he had taken in lieu of unpaid rents.

This struggle meeting was not spontaneous in the real sense. A lot of ground-work had been done before the cadres decided a meeting could be organized; the peasants themselves had to be encouraged to take an active part. In the main the ones who were the vanguard and showed relatively little fear were those who had fled into the city for work, became more sophisticated, and came back to their home village when they heard that the land was going to be shared out. These were the ones who were primed to start the ball rolling. As the others saw that Kuang was powerless to retaliate they too plucked up courage and began to accuse him. But it was necessary to live with the peasants, work with them and have long discussions, sorting out problems like that of Old Liu who thought the meaning of freedom was the freedom to be a landlord as well. It was a lesson to me because before that I thought I knew what freedom meant, but then I realized one can only measure freedom in terms of one's experience.

To most of my comrades the countryside and the peasantry were part of their own life. But I had to change my own philosophical values, to realize that for these peasants freedom meant a full belly, work and the fulfilling of basic survival rights and when these were achieved they could start demanding other rights which I had taken for granted in England.

Land reform was a fresh insight into how cruel Chinese country life had been. I listened to peasants come forward and accuse Old Kuang of cruelty and viciousness of a kind which I did not feel possible from such a kindly-looking old gentleman. But it was difficult not to believe weeping women who tore their clothes off to show terrible scars. One could not fail to be convinced when one woman described how her baby was torn in half because she would not sleep with Old Kuang. His defence was: 'Well, you should not have encouraged me. You took my present.'

As the day wore on the crowd became angrier until hysteria broke out and they had to be restrained by armed soldiers from lynching old Kuang on the spot. Afterwards he was sent to Peking and paraded with many other landlords and gangsters before thousands of people. Each had a board hanging round his neck listing his crimes. The crimes were read out and the question asked as each prisoner was pushed forward: 'Does he deserve to live?' The answer invariably was a massive 'No!'

Part of my steeling process was to attend the public execution which followed where 200 landlords and notorious members of underground '*tongs*' (secret societies) were to be shot. I still have nightmares about it. We were taken in a lorry to the place of execution, near the famous tourist spot, the Temple of Heaven. The victims were kneeling down beside cheap deal coffins, their hands tied behind their backs with wire. About six security police nonchalantly moved along shooting them in the back of the head. As they fell, some of their heads split open, some just fell with a neat little hole, while others had their brains splattered all over the dusty ground and on to the clothes of other victims. Some of the brains came out whole on the ground looking like the pig's brains I saw in a butcher's window recently, which instantly brought the horrors of the scene back to my mind.

Wang T'ao, who had come along in his jeep to supervise, saw me turn away in revulsion and start running. He chased after me, grabbed me by the shoulders and shouted: 'Take a good look, this is what the revolution is all about!' I screamed and wanted to hide my face, but he held me tight and twisted my head round and made me look. I saw my companions running over the bodies, cheering. Then, horror of horrors, Chang Teh-fang cheering wildly stepped back on to a body, its mouth opened and gasped like a goldfish. I gave a wail of despair, the ground began to spin, I reeled and would have fallen if Wang T'ao had not still got hold of me. He pushed me away from my shouting excited group and started walking me back to the barracks, telling his driver to go without him. I was thirsty, from the combination of the hot yellow dust kicked up by the bullets and scampering feet, from the smell of blood, from the cordite fumes and from shock. My mouth and tongue rattled like a stone. As we walked along the road, he held me by the elbow, talking all the time. I was in such a daze I did not hear a word he said. I croaked out I was thirsty. He took me into a shop and got me an orange drink. I poured it down my throat and retched it up as fast as it went down. He stood there until I recovered from the shakes, and then we carried on walking. We walked for many miles, while Wang T'ao gave me advice on how to regard the whole episode and what was the sensible thing to do. He said I was not to hide my feelings at subsequent meetings held to sum up our experiences and the inevitable 'thoughts' but should say what I thought because the criticism of my comrades would help me. We walked back to his room, I lay on his bed and went to sleep.

At our follow-up meeting I said it made me sick. I asked what sort of person was needed to calmly go around and shoot others in cold blood? I was accused of having the wrong class attitude, my revolutionary fervour was not strong enough. The men who carried out the executions were ridding the country of vermin. I was asked: 'What would your reactions be if you were faced with the same situation as some of the peasant women had faced in the past?' I tried to argue that there was a difference between revenge and cold-blooded murder. I supposed if my baby had been torn in half I might have cheered to see the murderer shot. Or was there another more subtle motive – to eliminate would-be antagonists in one fell swoop? That was only one public execution, but China is a large country and farther away from centralized control there must have been more horrifying executions. We were living in a harsh time. I was shouted down by hysterical men and women, the spit flying from the corners of their mouths, accusing me of being in sympathy with the enemies of the people, until I put my hands over my ears and pleaded: 'I'm sorry, I'm sorry! Help me to understand.'

'Auntie, Auntie, tell me what to think.' In an attempt to stave off the shock and the mind tearing agony I was going through I wrote a long letter to Auntie in which I poured out all my miseries, the killings and my longing for nothing more turbulent than the Methodist anniversary. It was like a pleading for forgiveness and the reassurance that she, too, might feel the same way I did. I then tore the pages up because with the unburdening came the knowledge that she, Uncle, chapel and Staffordshire were then nothing to do with me.

It was while we were engaged in land reform that the harshness of the times touched us directly. One night, an expropriated landlord crept into the temple where some of the men of our group were sleeping and slit the throats of four of them before another woke up and gave the alarm. Seeing those young dead soldiers who had walked with us in the lanes to protect us, who had joked with us, and one who had taught me to turn the heel of a sock I was knitting, I could have shot that particular landlord myself. But I could not call it 'revolutionary fervour' or 'having a correct mass line'. I was glad I never sent the letter to Auntie.

While we were in Huang T'u village the peasants celebrated the Spring Festival. There were Chinese dumplings. A tiny piece of pork is chopped up very finely and then mixed with vegetable so that the vegetable takes on the flavour of the meat. This is the stuffing for the dumplings made from another luxury – wheat flour. A tiny piece of meat thus feeds a whole family.

The boys in our group who knew how hungry Chang Teh-fang and I always were invited us over for a celebration meal, a special meal which included dumplings. They produced a magnificent stew – it was rich, it was fatty and for people who had not eaten meat or any animal fats in months the craving for anything greasy becomes an obsession. You even dreamt of fat lumps to eat. I used to dream of eating butter by the spoonful and slice upon slice of fat roast beef. Now here was this big pot of fat greasy stew and we all dived in with our chopsticks and ate to our heart's content. It tasted rather like old mutton and when we had finished we sat back belching and picking our teeth, Chang Teh-fang asked where the men had got the meat from. One of them replied: 'You know old man Liu's dog – the big yellow one? Well, he said we could have it, and that's what you have eaten.'

He was a very bad-tempered dog but did not deserve that fate.

These boys were not involved in land reform in the real sense of the word. They were there armed ready to step in and prevent anarchy breaking out among the peasants in the division of the land as well as to protect the landlord from an immediate lynching. One of the soldiers had known no other life outside the army. They were his parents. He remembered only serving as a little 'Red Devil' (boy soldier), growing up and serving as a regular eighth Route Armyman, fighting from the North down to Tientsin where he received two bullet wounds in the chest and was waiting like the rest of us to be found a place in some administrative capacity. His fighting days were over. He was a typical good trustworthy man who would be given every opportunity to rise in the hierarchy of the Communist Party. Once there was a great laugh when he came rushing out of the house where we were billetted in Peking shouting that his rice ration had disappeared. He had found a flush lavatory, thought it was a machine for washing rice and had pulled the chain, only to find his precious rice had disappeared. Another time a car had been sent for him to meet Mao Tse-tung; he was so impressed with the shiny black car that he took his shoes off and placed them on the running board before getting in and was mystified when he arrived at his destination to find his shoes had disappeared.

Our time in the army was coming to an end. 1 October 1949, was the date of the establishment of the People's Republic of China. There was great rejoicing, waving of banners and excitement at the Gate of Heavenly Peace when all the Chinese Communist leaders stood on the balcony and waved to the cheering crowds below. I saw Wang T'ao up there and cheered and waved my hands and shouted but the din was so great and to expect him to see or hear me among those thousands of blue and khaki clad people was like trying to find the proverbial needle in the haystack. I was disappointed because he had promised to look out for me.

Gradually the men and women I had lived with, with whom I had shared life and experiences, criticized as in one big family, left one by one for various posts. Some went on to higher education in the newly set-up People's University.

Some took over civil organizations that were returning to normal. Eventually only I was left of the original group. Wang T'ao discussed the various opportunities: I could go for more schooling at the Revolutionary College or join an English-language school, but the latter, he decided, was unsuitable as there were some 'suspect' foreigners there. There were half-hearted attempts at deciding what was best for me as my period of ideological training in the army was over. My Chinese was fluent. I felt more at ease speaking the 't'u hua' (common language) than I did in English! The army personnel knew we were lovers even though Wang T'ao had a wife and children in the North-East. He had left them there when the army fought its way to Peking and like many wives and dependents of active service personnel remained there until their husbands thought it safe for them to join them. In many cases the length of time stretched longer than was necessary when the officers met new faces and younger more desirable women. After the mass execution and exhausted with shock and crying I had slept on his bed through the night and woke the next morning cradled in his arms. I stroked his soft cheeks and traced down the grooves to his mouth where he kissed my fingers. His body was long and so thin I could encircle his waist with my hands.

I was content to let things be just as they were but he worried and once feeling low and depressed said: 'We must look at this problem with a Marxist viewpoint. If the Party says no, then we must turn another way and try again.' He took out his pen and a piece of paper and traced a line. 'This is us,' he said. 'If it's no, then we can go this way,' and he drew a line upwards, 'or that way,' turning the line down. 'But we must not give up whatever anyone might say. If you have the willingness and determination a true Marxist will always win.' I did not have so much faith in my 'Marxism' to think that approval could ever be given to a permanent relationship because the Party was beginning to clamp down on its members' forsaking their old wives and marrying prettier, younger women. Most of the higher echelons like Mao Tsetung had married beautiful young actresses who had flocked to the liberated areas during the war. When human relationships were more easy-going during the pre-civil-war period, Mao had picked the prettiest of four actresses and the other three had been chosen in order of hierarchy. By the time the fashion came down to the middle ranks the Party had been ordered to tighten up their morals. The Mayor of Peking was told: 'No, this is not the correct Party line!' and told to study Lenin's Glass of Water Theory. The neglected wives in the North-East had begun to rebel, and the Mayor with many of his colleagues reluctantly sent for their wives. I felt sorry for Mao's wife because the marriage had been highly unpopular and she was intensely disliked particularly by the army leadership. Wang T'ao always referred to her as 'that Shanghai whore'. They made sure she took no active part in politics but in diplomatic Chinese fashion suggested that looking after Mao 'was a full-time occupation'. I did not want friends of W'ang T'ao's wife to regard me in the same light. Already I received snide remarks from my colleagues and the deathly silence that followed every time we entered a room together made me feel as if I was in the same position as Mao's wife. I could not see any future in our relationship and while the pathetic diagram Wang T'ao drew temporarily lightened our spirits the problems seemed insurmountable. I was too shallow and young to think or plan that far ahead.

An English language news service of Hsinhua (New China) News Agency with its broadcasting unit of Radio Peking was now set up under a civil administration. In December 1949, after ten months' ideological remoulding in the Army I was assigned to help set up the English-language broadcasts, although I was still under the control of the army administration. I was eager to break out of the impasse and do something useful. As I rolled up my bedding and packed my few possessions, Wang T'ao stood there watching me. 'Do not throw dust in my eyes,' he said in English. I looked up, surprised that he should have taken the trouble to work out an English phrase. Over the past year, I had laughed at his attempts to learn English. I looked at him standing there, thin, projecting teeth and the deeply etched grooves running down the sides of his cheeks and remembered the first day I saw him just like that, except now I loved him. I got up and put my arms round him and put my hands under his cotton jacket and pressed his thin body towards me. He looked so vulnerable I wanted to protect him and be kind. 'We can still see each other,' I said but it was without hope. I knew that once I entered the News Agency, it would have to be the end. But I did not have the heart even to hint at it. In my short life experience had already shown me that once I went from one state to another all my links with people I loved were broken off. Don was in Taiwan flying again with the Nationalist air force, while Auntie and Uncle were part of my English hibernation; even for my father I had managed to find a niche – a faraway Shanghai childhood.

Wang T'ao and I continued to see each other in the evenings, and take long silent walks in Pei Hai Park. Once breaking a long silence he said almost to himself: 'She's still young. She'll find someone else and will want to divorce me. There will be no problems then.' The new marriage law had given the women freedom to divorce far more easily than their husbands could. I wanted someone else to make a decision, thus leaving me free of guilt and I thought if I saw less and less of him, time could ease the pain of a break. So we let things drift.

During the first anniversary of the establishment of the People's Republic of China in October 1950 we paraded through the Gate of Heavenly Peace. I was marching with the contingent of the Hsinhua News Agency and saw him standing on the rostrum. I stood still and waved my banner at him while the thousands marched past. I screamed out his name: 'Wang T'ao! Wang T'ao!' and thought; 'Now, if he sees me this time and waves back I'll fight to keep him.' My screaming-out his name became more hysterical as I realized my voice was drowned in the roar of the crowd shouting slogans and waving their banners. Gradually I got pushed out of the square and found I was crying: 'To hell with it, to hell with it, this must be the end!' I looked around for my group and found they had disappeared in the distance and I, carrying a poster which said 'New China News Agency', was marching among a crowd of cheering coal-miners.

Some time later there was an 'honesty and loyalty' campaign and one of my colleagues badgered me to confess to some crime as she was sure with my background I had some ideological problems to examine. But I could not think of any political misdeeds I had committed. How many can at the age of eighteen? All I felt guilty about was Wang T'ao and I confessed that I was still in love with him – a married man. They suggested I think seriously about what the implications might be. And because no one actively forbade me to see him I clung to the thread that he loved and needed me and therefore I loved him and he was mine. I did not need his sexual love, although at times alone in my bed at the Radio Station dormitory I longed to hold his body in my arms to feel his warmth and power. His fellow officers accepted that we belonged to each other. Life then was far less formal than later and the lines drawn between ordinary soldiers and officers were practically non-existent. His bodyguard who swept his floor, patched his socks and emptied the spittoon could nonetheless take part in political study groups and criticize Wang T'ao's work and attitudes. This general easy-going atmosphere was evident when Wang T'ao took me up to Mao Tse-tung who was chatting with a group of soldiers and said: 'Here is one of ours from England.' Mao smiled, showing his tobacco-stained teeth, took my hand in his and muttered: '*Heng mei li*' (very pretty) and then asked me if I had read *P'i K'e Wi K'e Shen Sheng* (Mr Pickwick). Wang T'ao remonstrated with Mao when he saw him light up a cigarette from the dog-end of another. Doctors had ordered him to cut down his smoking by half. 'See,' he said, 'I *am* cutting down by half,' and broke his cigarette in two. He picked up an apple from a bowl and gave it to me, saying: 'Take him away and share this apple with him.' With my young unsophisticated mind I took the attitude then adopted towards Mao by Wang T'ao, regarding him as just one of a group of revolutionary leaders which included Chu Teh, Peng Teh-huai and the heart-throb of all young army girls, the handsome mustachioed General Ho Lung.

The widening of the gap between them and us was gradual as China became more important. The next time I saw Mao was two years later in 1951; he was floating in a rubber tyre on a private section of the lake at the Summer Palace below the Western Hills, reserved for high-ranking officers. He had on a little white cotton sailor hat to protect him from the sun and looked like one of those nodding Buddha-like dolls which never fall over. He rocked gently on the ripples of the lake while a few strong-looking men swam up to me and told me to go away. I refused and said cheekily: 'Why, everything belongs to the people now.' Wang T'ao dragged me away and muttered to the men: 'She's only a child, she doesn't understand.' I was highly indignant and he pushed my head under the water to punish me. We watched from a distance while a few other officials sat in rubber tyres or splashed in the water, hawking and spitting and clearing their noses between wet forefinger and thumb. I did not want to swim any more.

Gradually more areas in the Western Hills became restricted as luxury homes were built for Party and army leaders. We were told it was just reward for the many sacrifices they had made for the revolution and so we did not even question the growing inequalities. One of my girl friends was married to a general who became Minister of Food and she took me to their beautiful home which had every conceivable luxury of a kind I had never known coming from post-war gloomy Britain. She went to it at week-ends only and during the week stayed in our dormitory.

Another time a group of us had been invited to attend a dance at the Tsung Nan Hai, part of the Hidden City which was the headquarters of Mao and other party leaders. We saw many well-known faces. We had to sit on chairs against the wall as they came up and took us on the dance floor. When the music was over they left us standing there to make our own way back. When we got back to our organization we protested at our treatment. We felt that this was a relic of the old times and said so in shrill voices. We had an apology and assurances that the Party leaders concerned were making self-criticisms.

Mao and the others disappeared behind the walls of the Hidden City and became remote and inaccessible to us all. When I saw Mao again it was several years later at a small reception for honoured guests; the band struck up 'The East Is Red and Chairman Mao is Our Saviour' and as he appeared on the rostrum the lights played around him as he strode slowly across our paths. A wide circle of grey-uniformed men made sure we did not get too close. They seemed short, emphasizing the tallness of Mao Tse-tung. The image the whole scene gave was one of an almost ethereal being who was not quite of our world. The circle of guards acted like a fence to keep us away. I looked on saddened at the scene trying to connect it with the one when he had told me to read *Pickwick Papers*.

6

Hsinhua

The Hsinhua News Agency was still in its infancy with a skeleton staff. It was housed in an old compound containing former stables of the imperial elephants. Another young woman, Wei Ling, was already there and the two of us were to start up an English-Language Broadcasting unit of the agency to be called Radio Peking. Over the next five years we increased our broadcasting staff to over forty personnel and finally formed our own department moving to the newly built Central People's Broadcasting Station, but for the first year we were just an off-shoot of the Hsinhua News Agency, sharing the facilities of the inadequate numbers of cadres who knew English. The Japanese had built several tall grey buildings within the walls of the compound. One was the office of the news agency while the others housed the hundreds of cadres who were to run the news service. Some lucky couples had a small room, but the majority of us shared dormitories still based on the army style. I moved into one with my possessions. A loudspeaker was blaring Russian folk music from a corner of the room. I was told Wei Ling would come for me and show me around but time passed and it got darker. The loudspeaker was now giving Russian lessons, unconsciously I was repeating the phrases: 'What is that?' (*Stoy edo?*), 'It is a pencil,' (*Edo karandash*), until I got into bed and pulled the quilt over my head. I felt homesick for the army I had just left and as I lay there in the darkening room the memory of the nostalgic gloom of Dr Barnado's Home came upon me. I was a new girl lying in bed among rows of other beds wondering what my next foster home was going to be like. I heard footsteps come into the room and peeped over my quilt. A sturdy-looking woman with short cropped hair dressed in a faded blue uniform stood looking at me. It was Wei Ling. She had a bright red boil on the tip of her nose and looked like an angry rhinoceros. 'What is the matter with you?' she asked. 'I'm homesick,' I said and pulled the quilt over me again. Some more footsteps entered the room and there was loud whispering. Wei Ling snorted: 'She's homesick, I didn't know we were getting a "false foreign devil"'! I sat bolt-up in bed ready for my first blazing row and saw a tall cheerful-looking man who grinned at me and said: 'Come on you false foreign devil, don't bother about her she's annoyed because you are to eat in number two canteen and she is still in number one. You outrank her. I'm Hsiang Li. I hear English is your mother tongue. You must help us because ours is not very good. Forgive Wei Ling, she has many personal problems.' He chattered on until the anger died away and I began to feel cheerful.

I could not quarrel with Hsiang Li because he seemed to be a person without any rancour, always cheerful and frank so that when he called me a false foreign devil I did not feel it was a personal affront. He was like a great big lumbering ox. His physical differences were explained by him being the son of a 'slave mother,' a poor peasant woman temporarily sold to a rich landlord in order to provide him and his barren wife with a son. When Hsiang Li was born and weaned, his own mother, whom he had to call Auntie, was sent back to her village while he was brought up by the landlord and his wife as their own son. He had inherited the strong tall physique of a northern Chinese peasant and he stood out among the more finely built, aesthetic-looking men of the Hsinhua News Agency.

The bad start between Wei Ling and myself was never resolved. We fought over every issue for years until our antagonism was part of our make-up. She was such an unhappy woman, rarely smiled and often cried. When I complained in a group meeting of her lack of friendliness and cooperation she admitted this was so and said it was because she was jealous of me. But it did not explain her general peevishness to everyone and the acceptance of it by the others. After the meeting, the deputy-head of our department, Huang Chen, took me aside and explained that I should treat Wei Ling with patience and tolerance as she had been through a very sad experience. Her American husband had been arrested as a spy, just before they had entered Peking with the Red Army. He had been an official of UNRRA who met Wei Ling and joined the liberation movement while doing relief work in Communist areas. She was finding it very hard to get over the tragedy, particularly as she had been pregnant at the time, tried to abort herself, became seriously ill, and in hospital lost both the baby and the ability to have any more. Wei Ling carried a burden which was hard to bear but she resented the gentleness and consideration of others. She carried a guilt complex which dogged her for years. The question was ever in her mind why she, a Communist, never knew the real truth about her husband and was supposed to be satisfied with the curt words on the day he disappeared: 'Your husband is an American spy. Consider yourself divorced!' She trusted no one and was suspicious of any kindness, regarding it as an excuse for hiding the real impression we had of her. She tried to prove her loyalty by working until she dropped with exhaustion over tasks that were relatively unimportant. She was vehement and bitter in her criticisms. 'It is not enough to read a script once,' she would say severely, 'it must be read ten, or twenty times if one has the opportunity,' and 'Why didn't you weep when Stalin died? Everyone should shed tears over his death.' But when she discovered that my father was serving a prison sentence for allegedly spying for the Americans, she was sympathetic because there was someone in a similar position. 'We both have problems to overcome,' she said sadly one evening, as I read her the latest letter from my father. 'At least you know where he is.' But the exchange of confidence was momentary and we were soon on a relationship of superficial friendliness but with a layer of hostility beneath ready to break out at any opportunity.

The establishment of the People's Republic of China had taken place several months before I joined the news agency and gradually the civil administration was beginning to take over from the army. There was still a transitional stage from army to civil rule. There were still three canteens, and the supply system with no salary.

My new colleagues were different to the ones I had left and

wore the faded blue cotton uniforms of government cadres. In the main they were former students who had escaped from the universities just before the rounding up by the Kuomintang secret police of those students with left-wing ideas. Most of them spoke English and I found it a change to use English after such a long time. They had been taken aback at first when I arrived escorted by Wang T'ao's bodyguard carrying my bedding and belongings. He had found my dormitory, set up my wooden bed, put a line over it and hung my still wet socks and flannel and then gone.

Li Mei, one of my room-mates, would have been beautiful but her features were badly scarred by pock marks. When she smiled she exposed a set of badly fitting false teeth. Her face had been smashed as she had stood in a lorry entering Peking for the first time behind the liberation army. She had forgotten to lower her head as they came through an arched gateway of Peking and had spent the first few months in Peking in hospital while her battered head and face slowly mended. She had lost all her teeth and had been given a set of UNRRA dentures. Occupying the bed on my other side was Chen Ming-t'ao, a big strapping girl who had an allergic rash and scratched all night. She was in love with Tung Mu-lan, a doe-eyed Shanghai beauty in the bed opposite and wrote her passionate love letters, until Chen's ashamed parents married her off to a distant relative. Thereafter we were continually disturbed by an irate husband hammering on the gate of our dormitory demanding his conjugal rights while Chen Ming-t'ao lay under her quilt pretending to be sound asleep. Across the courtyard was a large room for the bachelor members of our department. As well as Hsiang Li, there was Chou Li-feng, a son of a Kuomintang general who had become influenced by Communism at university and left to join them. He talked like an American gangster from the side of his mouth and liked to be called 'Scoops'. Huang Lung, a gentle Cantonese, was a Wordsworth fan, and when spring came wafted in and out of our rooms reciting, 'I wandered lonely as a cloud . . .' The only daffodils he had seen were in picture books. Wei Ling, my fellow announcer, was originally from Shanghai. She had been sent as an interpreter with an UNRRA delegation to the Communist areas and, together with Sidney Greenbaum, a member of the delegation, decided to stay and help with their propaganda work. These were some of the people who were my closest comrades in those early days of the Communist government. We shared the same dormitory, the food, laughs and sorrows until campaigns and political persecutions scattered us so far apart that we were like drops of water in a great sea of millions of Chinese.

Diplomatic relations were being established and with the forming of a new bureaucracy came tighter security regulations. Where before we could wander at will into different government organizations, visit old friends and dance at their Saturday night dances, there was now a clamp-down. The last time we ever freely went to another organization was one Saturday at the Foreign Ministry. It had a big hall and they had a good selection of modern dance records. We mooched to Irving Berlin's 'What is this thing called love', 'In the mood' and other hits of the forties. I wandered out into another room to ring Wang T'ao as I missed him dreadfully. As we chatted on the phone the door opened and Chou En-lai, the Premier and Foreign Minister, walked in. It was his own private office. I hurriedly put down the phone and apologized as he stood there looking completely deadpan. He courteously opened the door to let me out of his office.

Almost overnight each government organization took on its own autonomy. We had to sign a paper at the gate and be questioned what our business was. The insistence on secrecy grew to ludicrous lengths. It was impressed upon all of us that there were spies everywhere. We were issued with identity cards, badges and more identity cards together with photographs. I still have them now, a little faded but clear enough to see my name, my place of birth and my rank. We became suspicious of strangers and of each other, so that it was no longer comfortable to see each other, because it would mean a long report back on what we talked about and why. One became insular and only stayed within one's own place of work, lived among one's own fellow workers, shared the same dormitories, ate in the same canteens. Even the Saturday night socials were held within the confines of one's own organization. Friendships made during army days gradually faded away. Chang Teh-fang, my fellow drunken ice-skater, Liu Jui who helped me steal scraps of meat from the number one mess for my dog Hsiao Mee – the gaps between meetings grew longer. An exception was Liu Jui's wedding to a general who became Minister of Food. Liu Jui came once to visit me when I was ill with a bout of dysentery and brought a jar of honey she had collected with her husband when they visited an experimental state farm. 'This is good for your condition,' she said. 'Look, the bees are still in it!' In the middle of the sticky mess were several large horse flies. She was peeved when I told her so. One of the irritating effects of the new insistence on security was on the telephone. When answering a call, we were not allowed to give the name of our organization, the number of our telephone or even our names. So when the telephone rang the conversation went like this:

A: 'Hello?'
B: 'Hello.'
A: 'Who are you?'
B: 'Who are *you*?'
A: 'What number is that?'
B: 'What number do you want?'
A: 'Who is that speaking?'
B: 'Who do you wish to speak to?'

Answering the telephone was a little like playing chicken: who would give way first.

Secrecy grew to such lengths that often we found out news concerning matters within our own organization by reading about it in foreign newspapers, the source of the information being our own officials. When we protested, all foreign publications were censored and we were not allowed to see them any more. Starved of foreign news except what we read in the *People's Daily* or other similar publications we led insular and blinkered lives until what happened or what was said in the outside world seemed unimportant to us. The centre of the world became Peking, and this was reflected in the stories we wrote and what we read of others.

With recognition coming from different parts of the world the new China became conscious of its own position. In the news agency there were arguments among leading officials as to who would be more presentable when meeting foreign diplomats and guests. The head of the Hsinhua News Agency, Chang Hua, argued that he was better able to handle foreigners as he knew how to use a knife and fork and had met foreigners before and knew how to behave, whereas Huang Chen, his deputy, was too coarse and common, with his pock-marked face and tobacco-stained teeth. Admittedly, Huang Chen resembled a Chinese version of Jerry Cruncher with his hair sticking up like a bottle brush all over his head. But he had great warmth, charm and somewhere in his chequered career had learnt to play the guitar beautifully. He had humour and understanding of people and never once brought up their individual quirks in a meeting as an excuse for politi-cal criticism. The only person I ever saw him being unkind to was his own wife whom he did not love but was not allowed to divorce because they had an epileptic son. 'I don't want a wishy-washy woman like you,' he once shouted in a temper. 'It's like making love to a piece of fat pork!' In our dormitory across the yard we pretended we could not hear.

The clear-cut lines between the Agency and the Foreign Ministry had not yet been clarified and for a time the odd cadre would be whisked away from our office to fulfil some duty in an embassy abroad as countries began slowly to rec-ognize the new government. Their children were taken away from our own nurseries and crèches and put into a special state boarding school for diplomatic personnel. Once they left us all contact with them was broken, especially if they were sent to countries outside the Communist bloc. After they had finished their term of duty abroad, it would be another two years before they joined us again because they went to a special school where they were debriefed and any foreign habits and ideas they might have picked up were eliminated under constant self-criticism and self-examination.

Chang Hua got his own way and became the official hand-shaking functionary of the Hsinhua News Agency. Fulfilment of his ambition was short-lived, however. On his first mission abroad to attend a conference in Indonesia, he was killed in a plane crash. Huang Chen became head of the department, and Chang's functions as host and front-man were delegated to someone else who knew how to use a knife and fork.

I could not understand, at first, why so many of my colleagues were eager to work in the Foreign Ministry. It did not seem to fit in with the general attitude that we should be satisfied with whatever work we were doing because it was all important. Yet Yeh Chou, a French-speaking graduate from Shanghai, applied time and again to be transferred. It began to add up when I realized how very conscious of 'face' the Chinese are. One of the examples of humiliation by the foreigners that was brought up constantly was the old sign in a Shanghai park: 'No Chinese or Dogs Allowed.' 'Were you ever allowed in that park?' Yeh Chou once shouted at me. I could not remember but somehow I felt I was responsible for that humiliation. People like Yeh Chou wanted to work in the Foreign Ministry in order to meet foreigners face to face on equal terms and thus wipe out any feelings of inferiority. The loss of dignity so many felt they had suffered from the West in the past was more than compensated when they represented a China that was no longer the underdog and second to none. The over-worked admiration for the Soviet Union in those early days was easily reversed in later years to the natural antagonism now expressed. Yet then we so readily accepted that the Soviet Union was our greatest friend and ally that, even when after the war they dismantled Japanese factories based in China and took them to the Soviet Union, we thought in our naïve way that under Communism everything is shared and they were helping us in other ways. Perhaps if it had been left to our natural instincts we would have thought more of the thousands of workers put out of a job when their means of livelihood were taken away from under their noses. Wang T'ao was right in a roundabout way when he advised me to make my attitude to suit my face because that was how others judged me. My work was unimportant compared to a very humble attitude. A half-Chinese with the bluntness of a Midlander – that was an unfortunate combination in an atmosphere where such a mixture was, to say the least, jarring. Whereas Li Mei could complain about the bad foetid air in the broadcasting studios through garlic-breathing announcers and be praised for showing concern over the well-being of fellow announcers, from me it was regarded as contempt (*tse kao tse ta*). I learned to make my criticisms to a sympathetic ear such as Li Mei or Huang Chen and then sycophantically agree with the rest of our group when these same criticisms were raised through them. A Chinese trying to ape western-ized ways is an affront to dignity and I was called a 'false foreign devil'. This feeling of nationalist pride has become so ingrained in me that even now despite my British outlook I feel embarrassed and ashamed when I see a young Chinese wriggle and gyrate to pop music imitating his western coun-terpart.

The News Agency began to enlarge with Chinese students returning from abroad, overseas Chinese eager to join the new China. As the Agency grew larger, the tone and atmosphere began to change. They would come full of enthusiasm, dressed in their westernized clothes, like a breath of fresh air. Pretty young girls and handsome smart men straight from Shanghai universities, they were a contrast to us in our shabby, faded clothes. But as the weeks went by, they too began to be conscious of the 'false foreign devil' image and they put aside beautiful dresses and cut their curls; the men took off their rings and removed the gold straps from their watches and replaced them with a piece of leather or string. The fashion was simplicity almost to the point of rags. One could almost see the growing pride they had in themselves as Chinese and not as imitation foreigners. They spoke good English and were better educated than the cadres, who had mostly left in the middle of their university careers to join the Communists in the early unpopular days, and the easy atmosphere between comrades began to change to one of ambition and careerism. They were imbued with the western idea that technique and skill was the most important asset. The old guard argued that political understanding and a high level of political consciousness were more important but gradually the know-how and skill pushed the less able people like Wei Ling, Huang Chen, Hsiang Li and others into the background as they were made to feel inferior, like bumbling peasants. The newcomers were clever; they were able to master the complexities of Marxist jargon and turn it to their advantage at group meetings. They quoted huge chunks of Marxist–Leninist dogma to prove a point. It seemed as if the new China was going along the same road as the old one, with the middle class taking over the reins.

The old guard went on the defensive while politically inexperienced newcomers to the revolution began to appear as the spokesmen and influence the whole atmosphere of the Hsinhua News Agency. The slogan 'working for the people' took on new nuances as it became possible to 'work for the people' and have power.

The English-language broadcasting group was now headed by an overseas Chinese, a tall handsome Canadian graduate called Mark Li. Wei Ling and I were at his beck and call, scurrying behind him carrying his scripts as he strode majestically into the studio to broadcast the latest *People's Daily* editorial. I was confined to typing scripts and broadcasting non-political news items, because, he said, my political level was 'too low'. Wei Ling did no more real broadcasting because, he said, 'her Chinese accent is too strong and we must think of our image abroad'. I typed, Wei Ling translated, and Mark Li corrected and broadcast the scripts. Wei Ling and I were sandwiched in-between, reading out the wavelengths and signing off the programmes.

The newcomers were paid salaries, while we were still on the supply system trying to decide as usual whether our money would stretch to buy a handful of peanuts or the handcream. The resentment began to build up like a slow rumbling earthquake. The old revolutionaries who had worked before the setting up of the new government in the liberated areas of China had suffered years of deprivation and hardship. Now, with the creation of a new state, they were being pushed into the background while graduates from universities and from abroad were able to use their superior technique and their newly acquired Marxist slogans to take over.

The daily meetings grew more vicious. Sometimes the old cadres were on the offensive and the newcomers were on the defensive and sometimes the situation was reversed. A clear line was drawn between those who had joined the revolution before the inauguration of the People's Republic and those who had come after. The newcomers felt this keenly and at times it helped to check their upward course. I was sandwiched in between. Sometimes I was the target of one group, sometimes the other, occasionally of both. I was a little bit of everything. Because I spoke English I was regarded as an intellectual, yet was unable to take an active part in meetings which were held to criticize the faults of Chinese intellectuals, to make self-examinations based on a Chinese intellectual background. Mine was a unique position because, having come from the army, I held the rank equivalent to head of a department yet I did not fit in any neat little compartment that would justify run-of-the-mill criticism. Ever mindful of the mass effect of general criticism, no one could learn anything of any political value by my self-examinations because no one at Hsinhua had grown up in a Midlands mining town with poor colliers. The fact that my father was an American spy also did not help anyone else because I could not analyse my feelings towards a stranger whom I last saw when I was six years old. I grew to bless the former reluctance of my father to see me. So, not being able to stigmatize me in one camp or the other I was given the label of having 'a low political level'. I was used to being called names and I did not feel it was anything worse than being called a 'Chink, chink Chinaman' by people in England. Sometimes there was an impasse, both groups would then turn on me for my bourgeois attitudes. The complaint about fellow announcers breathing garlic fumes in non-air-conditioned studios was regarded as looking down on working people. 'How can you say you are working class?' they asked in a meeting. 'All working class people eat garlic because they need it to supplement a poor diet.' Wei Ling would question me: 'Where are the liberated areas in England?' and: 'Of course, people get arrested if they are caught reading the *Daily Worker*.' My protestations fell on deaf ears. Others would argue: 'The British working class are not true working class in the real sense. They have a high standard of living because of the starving millions in their colonies.' I was suppressed by Wei Ling's rejoinder: 'How can you portray the real situation in England – look at your poor mass line!' Because I believed her I never pressed the point or mentioned 'Uncle' with his silicosis and the floor of the outside lavatory covered with great gobbets of phlegm. It seemed another world that bore no relation to the cloister-like world we lived in. Mark Li, who had been born in the West could have enlightened Wei Ling's naïvety about 'liberated areas' and suppression for political beliefs in the West in a much more mature way than I could ever do but he always maintained a 'dignified silence' and refused to be drawn into arguments that were unpopular. As time went on, I looked more and more inwards, thinking of China, of Peking, as the centre of the universe, afraid of wanting to return to England because what mattered in China would influence the whole world. During the Korean war, in one of the many reports we were given we were told to prepare for a third world war. We dug trenches and went on military drill. 'Of course, some small nations will become annihilated with atomic weapons, but China's power lies in her millions and her vast areas. We will survive to reorganize society.' To us, in our enclosed world, it made sense. If I thought of England then, it was with pity. What a shame for poor Uncle and Auntie. When I mentioned that perhaps the small nations might not see it quite in Mao Tse-tung's way, Wei Ling said: 'Really, comrade, you still insist you have a working class background. Workers throughout the world are prepared for sacrifices!'

The intellectuals of China, then, had never come into contact with ordinary working people, as Chinese society was strictly divided, with no fluidity between different classes. They had an idealistic image of a worker, as a kind of modern saint. The government later took steps to rectify this image, by sending all government personnel, particularly intellectuals to do annual stints of labour reform. The thousands of years of Confucian philosophy of 'knowing one's place and sticking rigidly to the social pattern' has now been wiped out in a decade towards social egalitarianism. One early British trade union delegation who came on a visit to China in the first year of the People's Republic found it hard to live up to the image expected by their hosts especially as they were looking forward to a 'good old booze-up' with their Chinese fellow trade unionists. The height of hilarity was drinking a toast to '*Maisy Dung*' (Mao Tse-tung). In later years I got a look at my dossier. I found that the personnel department still stuck to the description of my grandfather, who had been a brewer's drayman in the East End of London, as a 'beer manufacturer'.

With 'Auntie and Uncle'

Married to Don, one of General Chennault's Flying Tigers

Peking Radio Pass, renewed in 1957

The certificate confirming that Cheo Ying had 'thrown off the yoke of illiteracy' at last

My dog, Hsiao Mee, before he was destroyed in the 'campaign' against dogs

Flag bearer at a Peking Rally

Friends from the Army

With Wang T'ao (front right) and friends in a Peking park

Overleaf Old landlord Kuang, with Shen Ping, facing the villagers

I was so convinced that I came from a bourgeois background and that I was a member of 'a parasitic working class feeding off the backs of starving millions in the British colonies', that my attempts at defending myself were half-hearted and I would go to Huang Chen, Li Mei or my peasant 'big brother' Hsiang Li and pour out all my woes. 'Never mind, Cheo Ying, take the good out and forget the bad, it's the work that counts,' and they would remind me of Wei Ling's troubles because it was mainly her continual nagging that got me so depressed so that I felt I was no use to Hsinhua. After such kindly advice I felt more cheerful and decided that the world was not such a bad place after all.

In 1951, another announcer, Chang Huang-nien, joined the office. She had just finished her studies in America and had answered the call to all Chinese students abroad to come back to help in the building of a new China. For the first week she and I sang American and English songs, spoke in English, talked about the latest fashions and records. We used to go back to our dormitory in the evenings with our arms round each other singing, 'Irene, goodnight, goodnight.' I thought life was much better for having a friend with something in common. But she soon dropped all her foreign mannerisms, put on the blue uniform, cut her hair into a straight bob and took off all remains of make-up. She married a fellow student, who worked in the Foreign Ministry. They were young and ambitious, determined to fit in. As months went by, she studied more and more, sitting up in bed pulling the bare electric light over her bed with a piece of string, while we groaned under our quilts. Most newcomers gradually evened out their enthusiasm as they became assimilated into our organizational routine but Chang Ching-nien was made of sterner stuff. At a meeting a few months after she arrived she criticized herself for being led astray in sharing her American coffee and pop records with me when she should have realized she was only perpetuating bourgeois habits and customs that should have been discarded when she left the States. She hoped the Party would pardon her faults but had not realized comrade Cheo Ying's background and had been influenced by what she thought was a politically more mature comrade. She said she was willing to help remould me and together we could throw off the shackles of a western background. She spoke so earnestly, so sincerely, some people had difficulty in restraining their tears. Meetings such as these had the tendency to become emotional where people cried and embraced each other over a good self-criticism. Wei Ling, in a voice choked with emotion, said she hoped that comrade Cheo Ying would take advantage of this generous offer and try to reform her bourgeois ways. The atmosphere was like some revivalist meeting with the congregation singing out praises as the black sheep was exhorted to come back to the fold. It had nothing in common with the type of genuine criticism and self-criticism meetings I had known among the peasants where discussions were concerned with issues based on real life in the villages.

If sometimes we could have laughed and joked during work and lightened that heavy cloister-like atmosphere, the physical hardship, the constant feeling of having to control what one said in case it was misconstrued and used in a subsequent meeting, would not have been so deadening. Ho Teh, an American Chinese, and I were skimming through a Russian magazine and started to laugh when we tried to copy the advice from the woman's page of how to massage and rejuvenate ageing skin. Wei Ling scowled and said: 'Why can't you read that very useful article on the woman Stakhanovite?' We hurriedly closed the magazine, fearful that our flippancy would be brought up at some meeting. Ho Teh and I purposely avoided each other in case we should be accused of forming a bourgeois-type alliance, and any free time we might have had would have to be spent in self-analysis. It was better not to form deep friendships with individuals.

Chang Huang-nien did not breast-feed her first baby and therefore made other nursing mothers feel guilty when they took time off to go the crèche in the same compound to feed theirs. She decided that she could do so much work if she saved on the nursing time. So for a few days she was in torment as she worked at her desk sipping a vile Chinese herbal mixture to dry up her engorged breasts. Poor Mei Li, who had just had her fifth child and depended on other nursing mothers to supplement her inadequate milk supply, waited outside the door so that Chang would not see her make arrangements with various mothers to feed her hungry baby.

When Chang's baby daughter became seriously ill with pneumonia, she continued working, occasionally wiping away a tear, refusing to take time off to see her baby. Wei Ling said to me when I commented on Chang's apparent lack of maternalism: 'Revolutionary mothers during the war were ordered by the Party to throw their babies in the river when fleeing from the enemy, so their cries would not give them away. She is setting a fine example.' The thought that nobody was fleeing any more only made me feel guilty.

She sat at meetings, quietly taking notes and saying nothing until towards the close of the meeting when she gave a resumé of the discussion, plus a few little political notes and lessons she had read from some Marxist work, summing up, as it were. It was always such a polished performance, so apt for that particular occasion. Exactly a year after she arrived, she asked to be considered as a candidate for the Communist Party, but she was told she still had not proved herself. So the sacrifices went on. She suggested that we gave up our public holidays and devote the time to 'give to the people', which became her stock phrase. When one of us protested, she replied: 'Really, comrade, we should be only too happy to give our time to the people.' With individuals like Chang, it was not necessary to force people to work harder. In organizations like ours, where intellectuals predominated, they tended to be more revolutionary than the revolutionaries.

One day she received an urgent message from the hospital; her baby daughter was desperately ill with kidney failure. She continued working but excused herself from the meeting at the end of the day. We were nervous and anxious and even Wei Ling begged her to go.

The baby had one kidney removed while her mother hovered outside the operating theatre.

In the evening I took some food back from the canteen so that she would have something to eat after that long day. As I entered our room, I saw her on her knees, hands clasped in prayer saying over and over again, 'Dear God, save my baby, dear God save my baby!'

'I've brought you some food,' I said and put it on the bed. She clasped me round the legs. 'God is punishing me for my betrayal. She must not die, she must not die!'

I could not feel pity then, only disgust. 'Don't blame him,' I said pointing upwards. 'Blame the devil.'

Next morning saw her back at her desk calmly working as usual as if nothing had happened. The baby survived.

Chang Huang-nien was typical of the type of newcomer that flooded into the new administration after the revolution. Like the others she was fighting a desperate battle to consolidate her place in the social order. She had to be ruthless. She had been born with the 'wrong' kind of family background – the middle class. She saw only too clearly that sooner or later, as cadres from working class backgrounds were educated to take over, people like her would be eased out to some backwoods post. She was using every means in her power to keep up front.

7
Campaigns

Every so often a mass campaign swept the country like a dose
of salts, and officials, writers, artists, people in the public eye
were purged and flushed out on a tidal wave of hysteria. Then
the criticism meetings and self-examinations were intensified
among the mass of government workers to pin-point anyone
who had the same ideas and sympathies as the people in trouble.

A campaign would start off in a small way: a cartoon or
letter in the paper which criticized a particular fault of
someone prominent. He was depicted smoothing his cheek
with a feather duster and then in contrast in the next cartoon
using the stick end of the feather duster to rap somebody he
did not like. This was to illustrate that when one criticized
oneself at meetings, one tended to use the soft touch, but in
criticizing others a big stick was used. Articles followed in the
press arguing on points until it gradually snowballed and
involved the whole country in the mesh of another campaign.
It gave the appearance of spontaneity. The campaigns were
in the main aimed at the middle classes, which also comprised
the intellectuals. They had been given long enough rope, now
it was round their necks. If they were not caught in one campaign, there was another planned around the corner. It was a
manoeuvre planned very much on the lines of a Chinese-type
guerrilla operation. The object was to draw the enemy out
into the open eliminating the opponents piecemeal. The same
tactics were used to draw out the intellectuals. They were
wholeheartedly for the social system because it satisfied their
nationalist feelings and gave them a pride in their country's
achievements. Objectively it was obvious that for the first

85

time in hundreds of years the scourge of poverty and starvation was being solved. The intellectuals were convinced ideologically that Communism was the best way for China and they were willing to sacrifice material standards and position but it was hard for them to give up their arrogance, their intellectual superiority, and this was where the most bitter battles were fought during many campaigns. Mark Li and Chang Ching-nien, members of our study group, were quick to take active parts in exposing their comrades but even they got caught in subsequent campaigns. No one felt entirely safe. Often it was a question of whom one could get into the firing line first to take the heat off oneself; but for many that merely put off the day of reckoning.

The Party leadership would criticize a few of its leading members and temporarily they were in disgrace. This process pervaded different organizations at all levels. For instance, in Hsinhua, Wei Ling was often the scape-goat because her actions and behaviour led to bitter animosities which needed criticism meetings to take the steam out of them. It served several purposes: it helped to stem Wei Ling's worst excesses and relieved the pent-up anger of colleagues, many of whom did not know her tragic background and were therefore less understanding. I wished I had been spared the knowledge of her American 'spy' husband but, because I knew, it clouded my judgement and laid me open to many of her irrational injustices. The others who knew nothing of her background and who had different motives and reasons for joining the News Agency tended in these campaigns to open their minds and thoughts when criticizing Wei Ling. With each campaign, more intellectuals were exposed as having 'right-wing', 'ultra-left' or 'counter-revolutionary' ideas. Wei Ling's 'crimes' were temporarily forgotten, while those who had been most vehement were in the firing line. They were asked to explain remarks made during the course of criticizing Wei Ling. Once exposed as 'right-wing', as 'reactionary' or 'bourgeois' these people were sent to state farms and labour camps in the North-East of China for a spell of manual labour in extremely harsh conditions. Yet they were still regarded as members of the original organization in which they worked. Once you were in a government organization it became your family, concerned with your political, social and general well-being. To be expelled from a government organization was like being turned out of a family because you were literally on your own. Where most places of work were government-controlled it became well nigh impossible to get another job. People dispatched to labour camps were sent for their own good to 'learn through manual labour'. During holidays some of them returned for a few days leave. Their description of conditions in which they worked were horrifying and I feared it as much as I used to fear 'Auntie' as a child in Staffordshire when she threatened to 'send me into service'. Delicate smooth-faced Shanghai women became hefty and thick-waisted with coarse faces and red calloused hands.

Wei Meng-chi was a typical example of those who in Hsinhua were regarded as in need of labour reform. She had graduated in English from a Shanghai university but had resented being sent away from home to work in Peking. She had hoped to study in America but the revolution had intervened. When she arrived at the office she did the minimum work required, took no active part in political study or self-examination meetings. 'I did not ask to come here,' she told Wei Ling one day who was trying to double her shift, and Wei Ling shouted at her: 'It is about time you examined your ideology!'

'There is nothing wrong with *my* ideology,' she retorted. When it was suggested that she should try to understand the contrast between her own bourgeois background and that of a worker from her father's factory, she saw no reason why it was necessary even to think about it. 'They had enough to eat and a roof over their heads. They should be thankful they had a job!'

She joined a clique of other Shanghai malcontents and they spent their time in the coffee bars and restaurants in the Tung An Bazaar. Gradually their criticisms of Wei Ling and her methods of work became more vicious. Wei Ling tried to analyze her own faults. They interpreted it as a sign of weakness and took courage to make anti-Communist and counter-revolutionary remarks. As they grew more vehement, others watched and waited. Suddenly, without warning, the tables were turned on them at one meeting. Wei Meng-chi was asked to clarify a point she had made in an earlier meeting. It was on 24 September 1957 that Huang Chen came and chaired our meeting. We knew something important would happen, but not what. By then I could simultaneously translate meetings and reports into shorthand which I found so much easier than my still laborious attempts at writing characters. The meeting was to decide whether Wei Meng-chi was a counter-revolutionary.

HUANG CHEN: 'The discussion today is not only for Wei Meng-chi but for all of us. Her wrong ideology should be brought out and if we can't get her to bring out her ideas today then we will continue the next day and the next if necessary.'

WEI LING: 'Last time, Wei Meng-chi said she doesn't think deeply about questions and after being criticized she can't enjoy life again. Why does she think like this? She must discuss this.'

CHANG KUEI-NUNG: 'Too much independent thinking affects socialist construction. Does this mean one doesn't have to think independently under socialism? Why does the leadership investigate people's history but their own isn't made known?'

HU MEI: 'I don't like to think about political questions but I think the real reason is that during the anti-Rightist meeting I found out my ideas were similar and so I didn't want to talk about Wei Meng-chi's political problems.'

YU: 'She doesn't like to work in political organizations like the Foreign Ministry, but she complained when she came here that no Party member ever talked to her.'

CHANG CHING-NIEN: 'What has been Wei Meng-chi's thinking during the anti-Rightist meeting? Her attitude to ideological remoulding? Her general behaviour in meetings is very active, she has lots of opinions but during the anti-Rightist meetings she never said a word.'

HUANG CHEN: 'Time is up for today. We have not gone deep enough into Wei Meng-chi's ideological problems. We must realize that we too can learn and correct our own erroneous ideas through this discussion. We will continue tomorrow.'

25 September

WEI MENG-CHI: 'I cannot use my old way of thinking to look at the problems of today. I do not have the same heart as the masses. I do not want to change into one of the masses. I am still on the outside like a bystander. I am a willing backward element. Sectarianism is a necessary evil because people are so complicated. I cannot understand how Wei Ling can get away with it. I still admire my American lecturer and remember everything he told me. He said the Chinese attitude to the Russians was overdone, but underdone to other foreigners here. He also said that the Chinese never talk to you in a frank way. They are always very polite, not like foreigners who talk straight out. He said he had a Negro servant who brought him up and he regarded him as a father. I am not the only one who looks down on the labouring classes, we intellectuals all do, that is what my lecturer said and I believe him. There are several classes now in China, let's not kid ourselves. First the Russians and so on down the scale. I always thought western democracy lets people do what they want and think what they like. Now I've been convinced through these meetings this is not true. On the question of my belief that the majority of the people are not interested in politics, I know now that today this is not true. But before liberation I thought differently.'

9 October

CHOU MO-YEH (*head of the radio station*): 'Wei Meng-chi is a serious case of an individual with bourgeois ideology. She has the wrong kind of thinking which is reactionary. Our struggle is being carried out in the Party, and among the people. If we look at it from the point of view of the labouring masses, Wei Meng-chi has bad and reactionary thinking. Her attitude from the beginning has been dishonest. She has never brought out willingly her reactionary thinking and let it be solved and helped by the masses. As Chiang Kuei-nung said: Wei Meng-chi's attitude is: "Outwardly I agree, but inwardly I don't." Wei Meng-chi is only just beginning to recognize she has serious ideological problems. Only just beginning and is also just beginning to realize she must change her reactionary thinking.

'We must take the attitude that if there is cause for reforming, we *must* reform.

'We are now starting an overall "*cheng feng*" (clearing up) to solve these contradictions and improve the style of work in the party. "*Cheng feng*" to the party and people is to do away with the three evils. Sectarianism, bureaucracy and subjectivism. There are still a lot of the "middle of the roaders" who haven't completely come over to the side of the masses. They all have different ways of expression. Wei Meng-chi is one of those who openly showed her Rightish tendencies during the "*Ta Ming Ta Fang*" (Great Airing of Views) period. She slandered the Party. She said one should look at Party members to see whether they are good or bad characters. To just look at that phrase is very suspect.'

His summing-up was the last word. Wei Meng-chi was sent off to labour reform at a state farm in the North-East. We had all expected more meetings and more of her self-examinations but the next day she did not come to the office. We heard from others in her dormitory that she had been told to pack her things immediately and await transit with a group of others to be taken away by lorry. Because she had tried to make some self-criticism she was not expelled from the organization, as in Mao Tse-tung's terms her contradiction was an internal one and could be solved in a 'friendly' way. Her reactionary thinking was not regarded as serious enough to be termed as an external contradiction and therefore there was no need for force. A decision about her future was deferred until after she had been for a spell of labour reform.

I heard that in a belated effort to avoid being sent away, Wei Meng-chi had married and become pregnant. Her son was born in the camp where at six days old he was badly bitten by rats and developed jaundice from which he died. 'Poor baby, it wasn't his fault,' I said sadly. Wei Ling shrugged her shoulders and said: 'Perhaps now she realizes the difference between a worker in her father's factory and her own life.'

I saw her only once after she was sent away. That was two years later; she had come back to Peking for the Spring Festival and I saw her striding down the road, big and tough-looking, just like a peasant. 'Where are you going'? I called out. She shouted back quite cheerfully: 'I'm off to the bazaar for a coffee!'

Campaigns varied in intensity. Some of them were socially useful, such as the hygiene campaigns. The Chinese authorities used what they regarded as the best available means to educate the people. Because of mass illiteracy, the only way to get everyone involved was to start up a mass campaign. Some had their amusing incidents; some were sad.

The anti-fly campaign was launched and everyone had to be armed with a fly swat. Children put a rope across the road to stop buses and cars and check that everyone carried one. Sweet, but it had sinister overtones which became evident in later years. We carried those fly swats everywhere – like gasmasks during the war in England. One bright spark in our office decided to set a quota. We had to swat ten flies a day, which was quite easy at first because China was full of flies. But when you have millions of people all involved in swatting flies they tend to become scarce. Posters appeared on the walls praising some activist who had overfulfilled his quota. We had to put our catch in match boxes and have them counted by the fly census officer each day. The rubbish dump around the canteen kitchen was a favourite spot. Another place was the public lavatory where there would be a score of hopeful people hanging around. Privacy was not much use if a fly entered the lavatory because it was followed by a group of fly-hunters each eager to swat it first.

I began to get desperate: I found it increasingly difficult to find my ten flies. One day while walking about disconsolately kicking the dust, I came across a dead snake. It was rotting away full of maggots. With a pair of chopsticks I picked up the snake and hid it in a box under my bed. I managed to breed my own flies. They were not ordinary flies but had a lovely golden blue-bottle sheen on them. I extracted twenty flies from the box each day and dutifully delivered them to the fly census officer. I felt a little ashamed when I saw my name emblazoned on a wall poster: 'Comrade Cheo Ying has caught twenty flies – gold ones!'

The snake kept me supplied until the campaign died down.

But some campaigns made me sad. The peasants were constantly exhorted to increase grain output and one day someone wrote to the paper to say that sparrows ate so many pounds of grain per week. The writer worked out figures to show how many thousands of pounds a million sparrows could eat. This started off a campaign to eliminate sparrows. As usual it went to extremes so as to get the whole population involved and make them conscious that grain and the output of grain were important. Therefore sparrows were regarded as a menace and were to be eliminated. The best way, it was decided, was to keep the sparrows flying until they dropped down exhausted. People climbed on all the roofs and towers, trees and walls, waving great red flags – they banged cymbals and drums for three days from dawn to dusk. There was a terrific din in which not just sparrows but all birds were kept flying and not allowed to land anywhere.

Peking was a city with many beautiful birds – the swifts coming in the spring heralded the warm weather after the long cold winter; suddenly they appeared gliding and swooping over the Temple of Heaven and the Gate of Heavenly Peace. The swallows skimmed in front of the pedi-cabs and donkey-carts. They built their nests under the curling eaves of Chinese roofs. There were beautifully coloured jays, finches and a host of other birds. They were all wiped out. The people were so carried away by enthusiasm they killed every bird on sight. I could not, would not, take part in the campaign.

Usually not a very active participant in campaigns – my 'low political level' was the excuse – this time I adamantly refused to do anything. Wei Ling said crossly: 'It is the order of Chairman Mao Tse-tung, you cannot disobey his order.' I replied with a Chinese army equivalent of, 'F – – – Chairman Mao, I'm not taking part!' Wei Ling was too shocked to think of a rejoinder. The slaughter of all the dogs in Peking and my shooting Hsiao Mee still filled me with too much revulsion to want ever to kill for whatever motive. I tried to defend the birds by questioning the possible outcome of disturbing the balance of nature hoping to start up some seeds of doubt in people's minds. But I was shouted down and told: 'The Party is always right, you have no right to question the orders of Chairman Mao.' I was the only one at the radio station who did not take part. I sat at the window in disgust watching my colleagues, some frothing at the mouth in excitement as each exhausted bird finally fell to the ground, was stamped on and crushed to death by a shouting hysterical mob. Wei Ling triumphantly picked up one crushed bird and threw it at me, laughing.

It was an emotional outlet for people who otherwise were kept very much on the straight and narrow, but our office was not able to put up the figure of 100 per cent participation; they had to make do with 99.9 per cent because 'Comrade Cheo Ying has refused to follow the order of the Party'.

The following year, China had a bad harvest. Fruit crops were poor. We were pestered with millions of flies and mosquitoes. Articles appeared in the paper blaming the lack of insect-eating birds and criticizing the anti-sparrow campaign. Now talk of disturbing the balance of nature became popular. I crowed at Wei Ling: 'What about that then?' pointing to an article in the *People's Daily*. She thrust the paper aside. 'I shall remember what you said about our beloved chairman. You disobeyed the order of the Party, that is unforgivable.'

The swifts did not come back for many years. I would look up over the Gate of Heavenly Peace and the Temple of Heaven and wonder what was missing in that marvellously blue sky, and then remember: the swifts were missing.

Wei Ling, in particular, resented my rather inactive participation in the campaigns and each time a particular movement came up and she brought up my blasphemies in the hope that the ball would start rolling, a directive would come from above to have a criticism meeting but it was not to go as far as a struggle meeting condemning me of political misdeeds. Huang Chen hinted that it was orders from outside Hsinhua and often when Wang T'ao and I met and we sipped tea, cracked melon seeds or boated on Pei Hai Lake I would tax him about his suspected involvement but he avoided a direct answer by saying: 'You are not an enemy of the people.'

The more serious campaigns were the political ones where philosophies were attacked. This was where the intellectuals were on the defensive. Well-loved men of letters previously established in history as patriots and social reformers were knocked off their intellectual pedestals. There were campaigns against the worship of western ideas and western methods of efficiency. In Hsinhua and the radio station this particular campaign was very strong. Mark Li was criticized for 'Big Shotism' (*tse kao tse ta*) and demoted to Wei Ling's job of translating while she once again broadcast the important news. There were campaigns against feudal attitudes, superstitions and beliefs. Among the superstitions were the religious beliefs. Where they were in the minority, these religions tended to disappear quietly and without much fuss, but the Moslem religion which had thirty million believers was left alone. It was not western-based like Christianity and therefore not regarded as bourgeois in origin brought into China by foreign missionaries. Most of the Chinese sent abroad to study had gone through church-run establishments. My own father, for instance, won a scholarship to England through his mission school. Therefore the campaign against the western-trained intellectual was double-edged.

We had in our office a quiet young girl called Sung Ho who had studied English in a Christian college in Shanghai. She was an inoffensive little mouse, a type that had passed almost unnoticed in our many meetings. Suddenly she was projected into the limelight as a typical example of Christian superstition. It was a glorious opportunity for the others who had used Christianity as a stepping stone to academic success in America and England, to prove how they had retracted their old ideas and to practise their newly acquired beliefs in endless questioning and interrogation of Sung Ho.

I felt then, there was nothing so rigid and heartless as a convert. The most vehement, dogmatic, inflexible characters were former Catholics. There was Chang Ching-nien relentlessly questioning Sung Ho as she stood on a platform with a placard round her neck, quietly and persistently probing her mind and thoughts over and over again in a kind of slow mental torture until I wanted to stand up and shout: 'For Christ's sake why don't you call her a lot of names and end this mental needling?' Then I realized that this stupid suppression was giving Sung Ho spiritual strength, so that she seemed to glow with a religious fervour that I admired and I wished that I could have that strength in a belief even if it was wrong, something to cling to in this spiritual vacuum, where no one felt sure of anything. Sung Ho regarded herself as a Christian martyr and the persecution only strengthened her.

She was incarcerated in a tiny room for weeks and told to write one self-examination after another.

We were forbidden to talk to her unless it was to persuade her to give up her belief in Christ. As the campaign died down and the post mortem began, she was quietly released from her room and allowed to carry on her work as usual. She made most people feel ashamed while they secretly admired her strength of character. She was an effective warning to all those who had secret qualms about their religious beliefs.

These campaigns were part of our existence in China, and involved every aspect of economic and political life. When China and the Soviet Union begun their bitter quarrel after the end of the Korean war it came as a great shock to everyone because before that the slogan was always dinned into us, 'The Great Soviet Union with the People's Republic of China by its side is leading the socialist camp to a glorious future.' In my mind the slogan was represented as a picture of a gigantic muscular Russian worker brandishing a massive fist with a slightly smaller muscular Chinese worker brandishing a slightly smaller fist. Russian was the first foreign language learnt in schools and other establishments. We were told in countless reports during the Korean war how the Soviet Union and China would be the industrialized nations leading the smaller Communist states who were to concentrate on agriculture. If someone suggested that it smacked of a new form of imperialism and had asked what other nations, including supposed Socialist allies such as Czechoslovakia and Romania, thought of the arrangement, we would have laughed in their faces. Of course, they must agree, after all, the Soviet Union and China were the greatest countries in the world. Our great Russian brothers were going to give generous help to China with machinery and other such aid. But when the Korean war ended Russia demanded payment for arms and supplies given to Chinese volunteers in Korea and said it was our war and not theirs. We discarded our warm Russian hats and coats as slight disapproving noises began to emerge against the Soviet Union in the regular reports given to us until it erupted into the deep rift between the two countries today. We had been so instilled with this 'unbreakable alliance' between the two great countries that

realization did not sink in for many months and then it rocked
the assurance of many of us when the insults far over-reached
the insults reserved for the American imperialists. It affected
the mass of non-politicized people less. One pedi-cab driver
said to me: 'They're all the same, these foreigners . . . always
out for what they can get.' For a long time we felt unease over
the widening rift because we had been so indoctrinated into
thinking that between Communist states there can be no irre-
concilable differences.

China was now determined to depend on her own efforts
and over the next few years the campaigns always stressed the
importance of China solving her own economic problems and
industrializing herself. Before we had depended on the Soviet
Union giving 'generous aid' in providing heavy machinery
and steel. Now a steel-smelting campaign began and in every
back-yard in Peking and the rest of China people started up
small steel furnaces. We all learned how to make steel. The
radio station, as usual, did it in its own crass way and we
found that we were burning more fuel and power than the
low-grade steel we produced was worth. As one expert drily
remarked, our steel was just about good enough to put on the
edges of vegetable choppers and then they would cost as
much as a motor bike was worth to cover the overheads. But
the campaign had its effect, the whole nation was conscious of
the importance of steel in industrialization. Iron railings were
removed; children pinched pots and pans from their mother's
kitchens to melt down in school steel-smelting furnaces. The
metal knockers on our door were twisted off and even the
tram came to a standstill early one morning because some
enterprising steel-makers had ripped up the tram-lines in the
night. It was a grand time for semi-officially approved vanda-
lism.

The result was a steel-conscious nation ready to back up
any scheme for speedily industrializing China. They were
psychologically prepared for the next slogan: 'Overtake
Britain in Industrial Output in Five Years!' and 'The Great
Leap Forward.'

Depending on the type of organization one worked for, the
campaign took a particular line. For instance, in the radio
station it was to present better programmes, meaning fewer

features and more political comment and fewer stutters. In factories it was to overfulfill production quotas ahead of schedule. In prisons a great leap forward in carrying out sentences. In hospitals European trained doctors and specialists were criticized for the western training which wasted so much time over operations.

A gynaecologist friend of mine, Li Li, who had done her training in England, was running a successful teaching hospital for training former prostitutes and sing-song girls in midwifery and gynaecology. Li Li became a target. She was shut up in a room and taken out at odd times to be struggled against. All the deaths that had occurred in that hospital due to self-inflicted attempts at abortion, miscarriages and stillbirths were blamed on Li Li. She was branded as a murderess, with big wall newspapers and cartoons showing her with blood dripping from her hands and mouth. From that it was but a short step to suggest that she was an imperialist spy sent to murder women and children. Li Li was pilloried and suffered because it happened to be that campaign and she happened to be western-trained so she must be the enemy. The countless times she had staggered around yellow and giddy from yet another blood transfusion she had given to a haemorrhaging mother while the husband and others stood by too frightened to give their own blood because the Chinese have a horror of losing blood, that was all forgotten in the venom and hate aimed at her.

A few weeks later she was reinstated. The campaign in her case had gone too far; profuse apologies from the Ministry of Health and Party leadership. They went out of their way to make amends but Li Li found it too difficult to work with and train the people who had so viciously attacked her during that campaign. 'I've had enough,' she told me one evening. 'I'm going back to England. Why don't you come with me?' But England still had nothing to offer me and I did not want to admit defeat. When I saw her off at the station I felt a little envy for the first time and wished I could have gone with her. But a strange feeling of loyalty kept over-riding that wish and the pull of Wang T'ao, and the thought that nothing else mattered outside China were still too strong within me. The individual tragedies and mistakes still seemed unimportant compared to the greater achievements.

'Write and tell me what you think, truthfully,' I called out to her. I wanted the reassurance that I was right in staying and she was wrong in going.

8
Hothouse

One of my favourite haunts in Peking was the Pei Hai Park, with its huge man-made lake, which froze in the winter several feet thick and made a natural ice rink. Wang T'ao often walked there. While he sat in a glass-covered verandah watching, I skated on the lake. Once while I was waiting for him in the nearby tea-house I saw a foreigner, an unusual sight in 1950, as most had fled before the Communist advance. He was a young Englishman studying Chinese in Peking who had stayed on. I had not spoken English for some time so it was pleasant just to chat about life in England and make the obvious comparisons while we sipped jasmine tea. 'So you're a "*Pa-lou-ette*",' he said. '*Pa lou*' was the Chinese name for the Communist Eighth Route Army and he had simply added the '*ette*'. I looked down at my faded khaki uniform and thought for a moment. 'Yes, I suppose I am,' and ran off to meet Wang T'ao, whom I saw looking across the lake for me. Wang T'ao frowned when I told him of my talk with an Englishman, and said: 'Never do it again. We are not allowed to have unofficial contacts with foreigners.'

Nowadays, I occasionally see that Englishman's name in print – a professor of Chinese.

As the post-revolution fervour became blunted by daily routines in the newly established state and society, foreigners from non-Socialist countries arrived to help. They came as teachers, doctors, editors of Chinese publications aimed at foreign minds. They formed a growing foreign 'colony' in a tiny almost cut-off world of its own. Problems developed peculiar to 'exiles' living in artificial circumstances, while other problems were very much the result of the effects of Chinese practices upon this group.

99

Among the first group of foreigners from the western world, as distinct from the Soviet Union and other Socialist countries, was a group of British, American and Australian Communists who arrived in 1951 in ones and twos to help with the English-language publications.

At the Hsinhua News Agency I had heard a lot about an Englishman called '*Ah Lan*', (Alan Winnington), a journalist who had covered the Communist advance into North China for the *Daily Worker* in early 1949, about the same time I landed in China and then had returned to Britain with the promise that he would come back soon. The office waited for him like a promised Messiah.

Wei Ling described him as handsome, tall and clever. I had a picture of some blonde Nordic superman. But she had also described her own husband in the same light and as far as she was concerned, all foreign men looked alike to her except where the colouring was different. She still had no information of her 'spy' husband's whereabouts or what had happened to him. She suspected he had been shot and in those brief interludes of intimacy when we exchanged confidences she described him as a curly-haired golden man. Brother Hsiang Li disliked the man intensely. 'A pain in the neck' he was fond of saying, a phrase he had learnt from me. From then on anyone whom he had the slightest disagreement with was 'a pain in the neck'. He even managed to get it into translations of *People's Daily* editorials when American imperialists were 'a pain in the neck'. I could find no one who actually liked Greenbaum and because of the general animosity he seemed to create, it was easy to believe the worst when he was arrested. Wei Ling was still morose and for days she had black moods when no one attempted to speak to her. Sometimes people asked how was it possible to be married to a man and not know he was a spy. At self-examination meetings this question was raised time and again until she dissolved into tears and said in desperation that romantic love had blinded her to his serious crimes, that her political awareness had been lowered, and she tried to find reasons for her mistakes. What made it so impossible for her to live down was the thought that she loved him and now had to hate him as all good Chinese should do, since the American imperialists were the Chinese people's deadly enemy. She felt she had to prove herself. So she drove herself and other members of the group to sheer exhaustion with unnecessary tasks, arranged thirty-six-hour shifts without a break, followed by study meetings, and then criticized those who complained of being tired. She suffered from TB and frequently had to stay in a sanatorium for three-month periods. Then we breathed a sigh of relief; life was so much less tense when Wei Ling was not there. She was intensely jealous of any newcomer, especially of all younger women who were married and had children. She tried to arrange shifts that clashed with their husbands' or children's holidays and if there were protests she reminded them: 'The work comes first.' Often when she was criticized for her over-bearing attitude to others, she broke down and wept and then for a time fawned on those with whom she was particularly severe. As the years passed and newcomers began to fill the radio station and Hsinhua, it became an unwritten law that her husband, Sidney Greenbaum, was a black shadow in her past, just like my 'spy' father. They would for ever remain on our dossiers as political question marks. A Korean Chinese who worked in the Korean section of the radio asked her to marry him but during those brief interludes of friendship resulting from another criticism meeting, she told me: 'He doesn't know how to love.'

'You should marry this Ah Lan when he comes back,' I suggested once. She replied: 'Not another foreigner. Look at me. Tubercular, barren and ugly. A fine bargain on the marriage market!' and she sank back into one of her black depressions.

One morning as I was preparing a script, the swing doors flew open and in strode a tall foreigner. Everyone rushed up with cries of welcome. Wei Ling, smiling until her eyes disappeared into two tiny slits above her laughing cheeks, turned to me and said: 'He's here, Ah Lan is here!' I saw a tall man, But handsome? No. He had a weak chin, a large nose and close-set rather foxy-looking eyes. I was disappointed. 'I think he's ugly,' I told Wei Ling and went on with my script.

There were quite a few English Communists working in the foreign-languages school and in the Foreign Publishing House but I had very little contact with them at first. Wang

T'ao's warning about foreigners was still fresh in my mind and the fact that every contact, even a mere chance meeting in the street or shop, had to be reported back to our organization. But then some foreigners came to the foreign languages press to correct the badly translated news bulletins. The quality of translation was poor because most of the cadres working in the English language organizations had learned English in schools and colleges in China and then joined the revolutionary movement without any practical experience in the use of English. Highly qualified graduates like Mark Li were rare in the foreign-language departments as many returning Chinese graduates had studied medicine and science. Mark Li had a degree in philosophy but the wrong kind as far as China was concerned.

A peculiar form of English which became known as 'Chinglish' was being produced. They could not see what was wrong with such phrases as 'Chinese women must support their fronts and consolidate their rears,' or 'Art-embossed candles suitable for the marriage chamber,' or, in a piece about the building of a new sports hall: 'Sporting lovers can now practise their art indoors in summer and winter.'

Such phrases made me laugh but when I pointed out the innuendoes they put it down to my low political level. What were needed were foreign comrades of high political and educational standards. I did not fit either.

To our particular department came an American called Sammy, from Brooklyn originally but who had spent some time working in Moscow and Prague. He was an aggressive, pugnacious little man beginning to get bald and fat. At a welcoming party he made a speech in which he said: 'I have no colour bar. All people are equal to me whether they be black, white, red or yellow!' Huang Chen choked on his mug of tea and went into paroxysms of coughing, Mark Li blushed red and muttered beneath his breath and I murmured to Wei Ling: 'He has a very high political level.'

Another arrival, this one from Australia, was Stanley, a veteran Communist in his fifties, who was highly respected by the Chinese because he had known some of their leaders in the days of their youth. He looked rather like a large pink elephant with his shining bald head which rapidly went a bright red in the Peking sun.

They and the others arrived with considerable misconceptions about what China was like. They expected it to be not only exciting politically but socially and, many hoped, sexually as well. They were installed in a small compound separated from the rest of the dormitories and living quarters of the Hsinhua News Agency. Each had an armed soldier detailed as bodyguard. Everywhere they went, the bodyguards went with them. I do not think there was anything sinister; they never stopped visitors and friends going into the compound, but it was a natural outcome of the sudden obsession for security. As the months passed, these bodyguards were seen less and less. They found it degrading to follow these foreigners into markets and shops and help carry parcels home. They stayed in their little room by the gate, reading, playing cards or flirting with the '*bawmus*' (amahs). They were demoralized but no one seemed to have the authority to remove them. Towards the end of the Korean war they volunteered out of sheer boredom and went.

We were told to make our foreign guests feel at home and in the first week of their arrival a party was held to welcome them. There was a dance in the canteen and the old records of 'Jealousy' and other post-war hits were played on an old wind-up gramophone danced to by Chinese couples in their stilted fashion with a space of about two feet between man and woman. Stanley and Sammy danced with the Chinese girls, who were all eager to make their international friends feel welcome. As Stanley bounced with a particularly tall slim girl, he made the usual small talk. 'Do you like dancing?' Then: 'Where do you live?' In her eagerness to make him feel welcome she offered to show him. Understandably Stanley took this in the wrong way. He went with her to her dormitory, where he made a pass at her. The girl, who had intended literally just to show him where she lived, set up an outcry: 'Rape, rape!' as Stanley turned pinker and pinker among the sea of faces that quickly surrounded him.

Embarrassed but polite, the Chinese smoothed the affair down, leading away the now weeping girl as Stanley realized that as honoured friend of China honourable he would have to remain. Later that evening there was a speech of welcome for Stanley and the others. In the Chinese text Stanley was referred to as 'our venerable elder statesman', but the unfortunate interpreter, not very expert, came out with 'our venereal elderly statesman'.

Hidden behind Stanley's back, I heard him mutter, 'Venerable yes. Venereal? Not a bloody chance!'

Until he left Peking Stanley never made another pass at a Chinese girl. Outwardly he appeared to be wholeheartedly the type of person the Chinese wished him to be: A good Communist, strictly moral, plunging himself into correcting English translations, a perpetual cigarette hanging from the corner of his mouth with a too small Chinese cadre's cap perched on the top of his big round head. But in private every now and then he stopped whatever he was doing, and cried out in real anguish: 'I wish I was in Bulgaria!' It was a lonely life. They had their own special kitchen and cook – a compound within a compound.

Sammy was his opposite. He was rebuffed, criticized gently by his superiors, but still attempted to make passes at Chinese girls, who all tried to avoid him. He had wandering hands. It embarrassed us because he was a 'foreign friend' and as such it was considered impolite to complain. At the occasional dances, whenever a group of girls saw him bearing down upon them, they scattered. Some unfortunate would be grabbed and – it was too rude to refuse – dragged on to the dance floor where he held her close tight up against his writhing body. One innocent girl complained that he should be asked not to wear his gun at the dances but leave it at home!

Sammy had been spoilt by the popularity of his nationality as a passport to the commodity-rich western world among many women in the eastern European countries he had worked in. He could not understand why he did not attract the same kind of response from Chinese women. Chang Hua had asked me to be his and Stanley's interpreter and general guide and often they poured out their problems and frustrations to me. I successfully repulsed Sammy's attempts to make our relationship other than platonic by saying that Wang T'ao, my future husband, would have a 'very yellowman's type' reaction. I suggested he used a deodorant because the smell of perspiration was obnoxious to the Chinese. 'Nonsense,' he said, 'it's a good virile smell.'

When he tried to drag Chang Hua's fourteen-year-old sister-in-law into his bedroom one evening, Chang Hua was so incensed that he demanded that the Party should either send him back to his country of origin or marry him off.

They were in a difficult position because Sammy had become stateless. In typical Chinese fashion they carefully weighed up and discussed the situation and came up with a middle-aged divorcee, Su Lan, who had lived and worked in the United States as a psychiatric social worker. It was decided that she was a good match and she was duly introduced by a third party. She was not beautiful; she had a long, pock-marked face, with sunken cheekbones, a pecularly-shaped brow with two large bumps on either side. She reminded me of a goat. But Sammy, subdued by the outcry over his last misdemeanour, found her charming and was deliriously happy. She was never known to lose her temper, always smiling and friendly. She had a good 'mass line'. She and Sammy were each able to give something to the other. Her long years in the States had given her a taste for foreign ways and habits which she could now indulge without being criticized for it. Sammy had a Chinese wife at last and his sex problems were solved.

Su Lan's continual smile and smooth disposition irritated those around her, and our faces ached with having to return the perpetual smile. She had a habit of glancing out of the corners of her eyes without turning her head. Although we all looked for faults we were unsuccessful. At nights we discussed them both trying to analyze the reasons for her wanting to marry that '*lao t'o tse*' (old head) because it seemed to our prejudiced minds no 'decent' Chinese girl would marry a foreigner. Often we looked round, feeling a presence, and found that she had noiselessly crept up behind us, still smiling. She was too good to be true.

One night as I came into their compound I found her listening outside the window of an American couple. I wondered then whether she had been intentionally 'planted' or whether she made it her self-imposed duty to check on what the 'foreign friends' were saying about their work and life in

China in the privacy of their own rooms. In this foreign colony she became known as 'creeping Mary'.

In a different environment, Sammy would not have contemplated marriage. He had wavered between staying on in China or moving to another Socialist country where there were less restrictions on one's private life, but in that artificial setting where one's values become warped and so 'Chinafied', she was a fitting companion who helped him understand Chinese ways – and assisted his political aspirations. It seemed that the more he missed out on sexual adventures, the more his political ambitions grew and his positioning for power increased. When he married Su Lan, he told us at the wedding: 'We will have several children – perhaps five or six – because Eurasians are so beautiful and clever.' She smiled and nodded agreement. They adopted two Chinese orphans which he grew to love but they never had any children of their own – beautiful or clever. I wondered what possessed him to leave his country and family and become a roving gypsy in the Communist world and then tie himself up for good in China. I supposed that, of all the Communist countries he had lived in, China offered the most exciting challenge in those exhilarating days when the future seemed so full of hope and promise and where people around infected him with an enthusiasm that other places had not. He once described how he had queued for four hours to get a wash basin from a Polish department store. China was a commodity haven for those people from other Communist states. We saw the Chinese department stores crammed with Russians, Czechs and Poles buying leather coats, pots and pans. Seeing those coachloads of foreign shoppers only enhanced our own feeling of superiority and national pride because such trifles as pots and pans, leather coats, and bric-a-brac were unimportant when all our basic needs were supplied by the state and the need for personal property was minimal.

As the foreign community grew in Peking Sammy's determination to be the recognized political chief of this mixed tribe grew stronger. He seemed to feel that his Chinese wife and his political experience in the United States and in Communist countries gave him a natural right to assume the role of spokesman for the foreign community *vis-à-vis* the Chinese.

Petty little quarrels and factions grew. Isolated in a sea of Chinese and admitted only to a part of the Chinese life, the foreigners grew frustrated. Minor irritations looked larger in their tiny constricted world, until one group would not speak or have anything to do with another. They were treated with respect and friendliness by the Chinese with whom they worked, but in the privacy of the Chinese's own rooms and dormitories there existed a world that was completely shut to all foreigners. On hot nights, when we could not sleep, we chatted and joked outside in the yard, drank green tea and cracked melon seeds into the small hours of the morning. One evening Sammy passed through. He sat with us and we all spoke English for his benefit and made polite enquiries about his welfare; the gaps of silence grew longer until one by one we moved off, leaving poor Hsiang Li and Scoops to carry on a careful stilted English conversation. This kind of invisible barrier exasperated the foreign community. There was nothing they could easily pinpoint and say outright was missing. Once an American couple complained that they were never invited to a Chinese home. A few days later there was a formal invitation to have a meal with a Chinese couple who had a flat. They went and there was a return invitation. Two pleasant evenings were spent. The American couple were happy. At last, they thought, they had taken a step forward through the polite Chinese reserve. It was several months before they realized that it had merely been an isolated gesture of courtesy.

Over the months, another rumbling source of friction among the colony of foreign friends stemmed, oddly enough, from the fact that a considerable proportion of the British and American members were of Jewish origin. Perhaps it was an aftermath of the anti-Fascist Left of the thirties and forties, or just pure coincidence, but whatever the cause, there they were in Peking, and many of them seemed to feel the need to make rather more of their 'Jewishness' in that cut-off setting than they were ever likely to have done in the countries from which they came.

To me, at first, there were just American, British or Australian 'foreign friends' with the only discernible differences in their red letter days. For example, some of them celebrated

Christmas and others Yom Kippur. I used to get invited to
both because I said my mother was Jewish. But gradually as
the antagonisms in the foreign community grew sharper and
more bitter so did the quarrels ostensibly between the Jewish
and non-Jewish factions. They accused each other of either
anti-Semitism or 'cliqueism'. Political back-biting developed
and individuals went tale-bearing to different Chinese
groups, who, in turn, tended to favour one or another group. I
was a bit of everything, interpreter on their shopping expedi-
tions, messenger girl and general dogsbody. I was willing to
be used because it gave me pleasure to be with English-
speaking people yet still stand apart and go back to my
Chinese 'family'. They acted as a safety valve to my pent-up
emotions. I ate gefilte fish with the Jewish comrades and tripe
and onions and hamburgers with the others. I saw the advantages of the old imperialist ploy of divide and rule in this
small foreign community, remembering from my Shanghai
childhood the hated Sikh policemen cracking truncheons on
Chinese heads while the British officer sat behind his desk
and played at being 'fair'. Now it was the turn of the Chinese
to sit back and manipulate the divided groups. We were
unaware that already there was a split in the Chinese party
between the extreme left which favoured the Jewish group of
foreigners and the so-called moderate or as they became later
the capitalist roaders who favoured the non-Jewish foreigners.
Wang T'ao appeared distant and ill at ease, not wanting to
discuss the political events influencing Party decisions and he
disappeared for months on end to the North-West of China
when the only sign that he still thought of me were the occasional parcels of goodies that were delivered by a soldier colleague and once a beautiful fur Cossack army hat with the
curt instruction from the messenger: 'Comrade Wang T'ao
says to look after your health!' It seemed as if the army did
not want to become involved in the positioning of power and
politics and were staging a waiting game.

Wang T'ao had his permanent quarters at the old Tartar
city of Peking but flew backwards and forwards to the North-
West of China, Sinkiang, where he was in charge of the
national minorities. He brought back groups of Cossacks,
Uighurs and Uzbeks – handsome tall men to be trained as

future officers and cadres. They were so unlike the Hans, often with blonde hair and blue eyes, Russian-speaking and pro-Russian. They taught me Russian folk dances and they were far more eager to learn to speak English than Chinese. Wang T'ao angrily told me to stop. 'They are here to learn to become Hans.' I was no longer allowed to eat in the common mess but had to eat with Wang T'ao and his colleagues in the officers' mess and he forbade any further contact with them.

As the government campaigns developed some of the foreigners insisted on becoming involved. Their speeches and criticisms were listened to politely and, if they insisted inordinately, some form of mild criticism was returned. It became a source of rivalry to demonstrate which group was the most 'politically active'.

While Stanley was in Peking, he was able to contain some of the worst excesses of the various factions. As the 'venerable elder statesman' and by sheer force of personality he kept the foreigners outside Chinese politics. 'We're here as technicians,' he would say firmly to people like Sammy who were desperate to be involved more fully into Chinese life. But when Stanley's contract expired he resisted the invitation to stay on for two more years and returned to Australia and from there went to his beloved Bulgaria, where he finally married his gorgeous Bulgarian. Sammy had lost his American passport and nationality due to American law at that time and so was unable to return to the United States. This rejection no doubt made him eager to belong to something. He took on an air of martyrdom; 'I have lost my country for China,' he once told us. He began to invite different officials to cosy little dinner parties at his flat, where his very presentable wife spiced the menu with scraps of information she had gleaned from servants working with other foreigners. To outsiders, it seemed unimportant and trivial, but for those living in the claustrophobic isolation of these 'foreign friends' the atmosphere became tense and fraught with suspicion.

Sammy had the habit of keeping a little notebook in which he wrote down what people said and did. Then, when the right campaign arrived, he got his wife to write up a big wall newspaper quoting word for word or deed by deed what had been said and done even two or three years before. For instance, in a campaign for economy, a wall newspaper went up about one of his greatest rivals, a fellow American who worked hard but also believed in playing hard. He enjoyed a drink, a good meal and holding parties in his home. Two years previously he had celebrated his fortieth birthday and invited the whole office to a party. Sammy criticized the extravagance and arrogance of celebrating one's own birthday 'when we should economize to make our country strong'. He was also careful to criticize himself for celebrating Jewish festivals which were religious in origin and therefore incompatible with being a good Communist. He made us all feel terribly guilty for taking part in that birthday extravagance particularly as the nation was in the throes of an economy campaign, albeit two years later!

Such persistent grinding down of particular victims became an obsession for Sammy. He was given the nick-name of 'The Blivet', coined by an American doctor who defined it as: 'Two pounds of shit in a one-pound bag.' During an anti-bourgeois literature movement, Sammy spoke censoriously of the fondness of many in the foreign group for paperback detective novels. Well-thumbed Agatha Christies were passed from addict to addict. Making a collective self-criticism at one meeting, Sammy said: 'We foreign comrades must also examine our motives in reading bourgeois detective novels.' He went on at great length criticizing himself for reading bourgeois trash and promising that in future he would only read the works of working-class authors such as Mark Twain and Charles Dickens. He reminded me of a Communist Uriah Heep in his 'umbleness and my feelings of pity became tinged with active dislike.

Looking at these strange people, I felt deep down they were desperately unhappy, unable to settle in their own countries, leading restless lives running away from themselves, always seeking solutions in different environments. I pushed down the thought that some of those characteristics may have been mine. It was a great pity that, unlike Stanley, they were not encouraged to return to their own countries after their contracts were over. Instead the enclosed life of China had seeped into their beings and made them into misanthropes; they bore no relation to people like my Staffordshire family, Auntie and

Uncle, whom I felt these foreigners would look on with contempt and censure.

Occasionally Sammy was rewarded by being invited to an official function where he had the opportunity of shaking some dignitary's hand, or was taken to meet some important personage arriving at the airport. On return, he reported his meetings to the rest of the foreign group, saying: 'See this hand? It's actually held so and so's hand. I'm not going to wash it for a week!' He regarded these occasions as official approval for his bid for leadership of the foreign community. But despite all his efforts he earned scant respect from his Chinese colleagues who occasionally made sly digs about his behaviour, though he served a purpose and was rewarded like a tame pet for each trick. Foreigners were kept under control by being rewarded with special favours if they had done something well and ignored if they had not. This Pavlovian approach seemed to extend to visiting statesmen, even in later years with presentations of rich gifts.

Alan skimmed round the edges of the foreign community. His position as a journalist working for a left-wing paper gave him an ambivalent position. His ties with his paper abroad gave him the independence which the others did not have. In the early years he could wander at will into the Hsinhua News Agency offices and see what news there was, flirt with the girls and make Wei Ling happy for the day if he talked with her or send her into depths of despair if he did not.

I liked Alan for his independent outlook and lack of conformity, because he spoke outright about the faults and mistakes we made in our work. I felt of all those foreigners he was the least hypocritical. He seemed to sense the psychological turmoil as I tried to suppress all things English yet missing the opportunity of talking and behaving like other English girls. Often when I had been hauled over the coals for another misdemeanour such as losing my temper – 'So barbarian, comrade' – I went and sat in his flat and fumed or cried as the case might be, while he made me a cup of English tea and calmed me down. Once he said: 'You're pretending to be a Chinese girl, but really you are as English as I am.' I shouted 'I'm not! I'm not!' and stormed out, determined never to visit these foreigners again. For a time I was content with my

Chinese life and felt part of it again, only to miss the companionship these foreigners offered. Alan dubbed himself my 'Dutch uncle' and would say: 'Tell me all about it.' It was difficult to unwind and really say what I thought about my organizational life; there was always a reserve which seemed to stop me from committing myself too much to anyone. The emotional tie to Wang T'ao and his injunction never to trust foreigners was too ingrained in me even despite my admiration for Alan to expose that little part of my Chinese life. So I would skim around my apprehensions, my confused emotions and take comfort in a cup of English tea and talk about England instead.

After the death of Stalin, Sidney Greenbaum suddenly appeared in the office and was introduced to the staff as 'our new American comrade who is a member of the Chinese Communist Party'. Wei Ling had been particularly morose over the past few weeks and at night as we lay in our dormitory we could hear her crying. We could not comfort her as she had always spurned any kindly overtures. I felt so very sorry when I thought of her agony because in those unguarded moments when we did talk about our past, I could feel she loved Sidney Greenbaum so much that it poisoned her view of life. I tried to be kinder but it was such an uphill job. Two weeks previously she had suddenly married the Korean Chinese Lao Feng, yet had made no effort to get a separate room. We thought it was just another expression of her warped outlook and left her alone.

The pieces now fitted. She had given Greenbaum a way out as she could not have children and he wanted a family to make up for the lost years he had spent in prison.

Greenbaum married a healthy, rather cow-like peasant woman. It was a typical marriage ceremony. We made an apple-pie bed, hid dolls and baby's dummies around the room and teased the pair. He asked for a woven portrait of Chairman Mao as a wedding present from us. Wei Ling stayed away.

From then on Greenbaum's new wife produced child after child in rapid succession. It was as if he was making up for lost time. He wore the shabby uniform of a Chinese cadre, hawked and spat like a peasant – a strange-looking Chinese

112

with American features. He was flabby and had lost his curly blonde hair, spoke English with a Chinese accent and had as much humour as a wet Chinese blanket.

We all begged Huang Chen to arrange a transfer for Wei Ling but were told that the experience could be regarded as a steeling process in becoming a good Communist Party member while Greenbaum offered to 'help' her in overcoming her ideological problems. Once I found her crying alone in the dormitory and a cold, expressionless Greenbaum stalking away. 'I'm mad, I must be,' she told me. 'You have to excuse my bitterness towards you. It is not really me. It is my madness that struggles to overcome my correct attitude towards you.'

She moaned and rocked herself backwards and forwards, her arms crossed over her breasts as if she was in pain. I cried for her and foolishly hinted at what Wang T'ao had told me. I had mentioned Greenbaum as an innocent victim of Stalin, only to be told: 'Not so innocent. His time will come again!' Then I found the two allied against me in a vendetta of hatred. I could not hate Greenbaum, but I feared him. He had so much power over us, partly because Hsinhua wanted to make up for past injustices. Even Huang Chen, the head of Hsinhua, seemed nervous and unsure of his position in his presence, and this atmosphere seeped through to all of us. We could not hate him, he was like a being devoid of all human emotion and response. He carried the Chinese phlegmatism to such an extreme that he surpassed them all. He stared at you with vacant blue eyes and you felt he was not a human being at all but some part of a machine and the sentence you were in the middle of saying tapered off and froze in mid-air. We idly speculated whether he even enjoyed making love for he never seemed to speak to his wife. But the babies kept coming with unfailing regularity. Romantically I sometimes pictured a time when Greenbaum had fathered enough children – 'Another son', he would proclaim, 'to fight against the Americans!' – and when he had built up his 'army', he and Wei Ling would be together again. 'A good Marxist will always find a way,' Wang T'ao had said. But that was fanciful. In real life they were united in making my life and that of Ho Teh, my fellow announcer, unbearable. Ho Teh went

113

back to America sadly disillusioned, two years after Greenbaum returned, hating him, Wei Ling and China. Sammy and Sidney were for a time locked in a bitter positioning for power, but Sidney could think and talk like a Chinese and the added advantage of the Chinese trying to make up for the past injustices helped him to achieve extra points. After his imprisonment, he was admitted into the Chinese Communist Party – a rare achievement for a foreigner, but then he was not a foreigner. He was in essence a Chinese. It was if they had taken his guts and his brain, refashioned them and covered it all by a flabby white skin.

After this first disappointment, Sammy joined forces with Sidney Greenbaum in leading the foreign community and acting as guardians of their moral and political education. Sammy applied to become a Chinese citizen and also to become a member of the Party. The two of them now joined in 'purging' the foreigners, getting sent home those who they persuaded the Chinese authorities were undesirables.

The 'Foreign Friends' were now placed in a rapidly emptied special village several miles outside Peking which had previously housed the Russian advisers and their families. There they were walled in from the rest of China. Within those walls they had their own social life, shops, schools and restaurants. It was called the 'Friendship Village' but others called it the 'Foreign Ghetto' or 'The Forbidden City'. To try to enter to see friends or acquaintances meant going through formalities which made British immigration-control measures look easy.

The heady years of the revolution were now being succeeded by humdrum years which were to be enlivened by intense campaigns decreed from above, in which many good people suffered, often for no good purpose. Ironically Wang T'ao's prediction came true. Years later, Sammy and Sidney themselves suffered punishment and degradation – in part for the conspiratorial web they had themselves woven.

9

Ming Tombs

From the north of China right down to Peking sweeps the great flat North China plain, denuded of forests, vegetation and water. In the summer Peking suffers six weeks of continuous rain, perhaps the only rainfall of the year. The climate is so dry that even the snow falling in winter comes down like fine yellow dust. A famous local delicacy is called Peking Dust; a powdered chestnut topped with whipped cream. 'Peking Throat' is a sore dry inflammation which is alleviated by the old peasant remedy of eating slices of sweet raw turnip. Eyes get itchy, red and sore. The dreaded '*sar yen*', tracoma, was so common that many caught it in some mild form or another and needed treatment. In the early days, before the Government was established, there used to be a paper boy of about twelve standing at the entrance to the Tung An Bazaar, selling papers all day. I noticed one morning his eyes were pink and runny. The next day he was still there, his eyes more red and he rubbed them frequently. I was curious and asked Wang T'ao: 'Why doesn't he get treatment from the doctor?' He smiled and said: 'You have a lot to learn. Millions need doctors. That's why you and I are wearing this uniform.' He went on with the much-used phrase '*Yi bu yi bu*' (step by step) and he gave me a long lecture on what the revolution really meant. I was stubborn and argued that this boy was right under our noses. 'Why can't we go to the chemist and at least buy some ointment?' Wang T'ao put on an air of injured superiority: 'Your bourgeois humanitarianism is coming up to the surface again.' So every day I passed him still selling newspapers and observed his eyes getting worse. I then went off to land reform and did not return to Peking for several months. I passed him once again. This time, his inner lids

115

had turned outwards in a red raw mess. His eyeballs were turned towards the sky seeing nothing. He was blind and he was still selling newspapers.

The yellow dust penetrated every nook and cranny, drying out the glass panes from unseasoned wood of modern buildings until they fell with a sob of splintering glass.

Peasants walked alongside their donkey carts shovelling up the dust in the lanes enriched by city travel, to take back to the thin soil from whence it came. Dust lodged permanently in the corners of our eyes and nostrils, a sheen of yellow dust on our faces and clothes. We automatically blew the layer of dust away from the surface of the mugs of hot water before we drank and it collected like tidal drifts on the inside of the mug. The sun shone through a yellow haze, drying wet clothes so quickly that they became stiff and hard like cardboard. Rickets was common among undernourished children, despite the continuous sunshine. Li Mei's children were bow-legged, their arms like little chopsticks with big misshapen heads. When she took them to a Russian specialist he claimed there was a permanent dust cloud over Peking which filtered the ultra violet and therefore her children were unable to receive the bone-hardening rays of pure sunshine.

We dashed water against our faces, rinsing and rinsing, not daring to rub, as the dust acted like sandpaper and made our faces smart as if they had been in a Siberian winter wind again. We dreaded the March winds. We ate dust, we breathed dust, we smelt dust until it became part of our existence.

Then, sometime in July and August, the rains came making the lanes and streets of Peking ankle deep in slushy mud and the yellow flat plains ouside the city walls became muddy swamps, evil smelling and vile. At first we welcomed the rain and splashed and revelled in the lanes but cloth shoes are not meant for the wet so they turned into rotting lumps of rag, foul-smelling because of the fish glue used to stick the soles together. Once, before the dogs were taken away, I saw a puppy lying ill in a puddle of mud by the steamed dumpling stall; it shivered and shook for three days before it died.

Then, just as suddenly as the rains came, they ceased again. The lanes dried up and Peking once again became a city of dust.

The Japanese were blamed for cutting down all the trees during the war but Peking dust had been a scourge for centuries. Articles began to appear in the press emphasizing the need for mass campaigns for afforestation and water conservation. Schools, colleges and organizations were mobilized to plant trees. We all planted trees in the outskirts of Peking. We covered bare hills with tiny saplings cutting semi-circular holes into the sides of the hills which from a distance looked like the scaly body of a huge fish.

Later we formed part of a mass mobilization of intellectuals to have their first taste of manual labour in the building of a dam, to collect this massive yearly rainfall and store it in a gigantic reservoir near the Ming Tombs.

The Ming Tombs lie a few miles outside the city of Peking. There the emperors of the Ming dynasty and their families were buried. The burial chambers were hidden among a collection of artificial hills, bare and ugly, a few rounded mounds of yellowed grass. This was where the reservoir was planned to help irrigate mile upon mile of the dusty-yellow soil around the Ming Tombs.

Chinese intellectuals used to wear long fingernails to prove they never worked with their hands but with their minds. In our office, the habit was to grow the little fingernail as long as possible. It was a cult, because there was still an inborn contempt for working with one's hands. The cadres of peasant–worker stock, once they entered government office and became 'contaminated' with this feudal habit, also grew their little fingernails and pretended they did not know how to handle a broom, or use a hammer; it was all a great act to show the ingrained contempt for manual work.

Groups of people from the radio station were sent to the Ming Tombs Reservoir site to help with the digging. Thousands of people were needed to form a voluntary work force to dig out the hills and carry the earth several miles away to the dam site. All government organizations in Peking were sending groups of their people in turn. As each group from the radio station returned after their three-week stint, they protested that they did not want to come back; they loved labour. But their appearance belied their protests; they looked weary, tired and wretched, and secretly relieved that their course of labour reform was over and they could sink back into the relative comfort of office life. To our enquiries the comment was '*heng k'u*' – very bitter. Some had been sent to hospital suffering from exposure and exhaustion. We all fretted, nervously waiting for our turn and making a great show of disappointment when our name did not appear on the list.

Our turn finally came. We were told to take our bedding, a mug, wash basin and flannel and our inevitable notebook to write up our experiences and self-criticism. As I got my things together and left my few accumulated luxuries, I thought: 'Here we go again. It's just like the army!'

We were billeted in a tiny hamlet just over four miles from the actual site. A former landlord's old tumble-down house had been reserved for the fifty radio station members. Our English section included a former newscaster from the BBC foreign-news service, Chang Su-san. She and her husband had returned to the new China from relative comfort and security in London for the sake of their children's future, not because they were politically inspired. As soon as their children started in Chinese schools, they began to indoctrinate their parents and criticize them for their lack of interest in politics. One day, Chang Su-san invited me to her very pleasant house for English tea. She still tried to cling to some standards of English comforts, but eventually even she moved out to the government dormitory while her husband stayed with the Foreign Languages Press and her children went to state boarding schools.

As we sipped our Earl Grey tea, her nine-year-old daughter burst in and stared at us in disgust. We guiltily put down our cups and waited for the tirade.

'How can you sit there so unconcerned, when the American imperialist dogs are supporting the Kuomintang lackeys in Taiwan? Taiwan belongs to China!' She raised her little fist and dashed out of the room: 'We must unite to drive the American aggressor from Chinese territory!'

Chang Su-san looked at me and sighed:

'I hear this all day,' she said. 'Politics, politics, I'm sick of politics. They won't even eat chips any more, they say it is bourgeois.'

Now, this delicate middle-aged woman with her rimless

spectacles and permed hair, sat with me after a dusty lorry ride from Peking. We were yellow with dust from head to foot. She wiped the dust from her spectacles, and tried to brush it away from her clothes. She had never given in to the sloppy untidy fashion of wearing the clothes so popular among the new government cadres. She always looked smart and neat by cutting and reshaping the baggy blue jacket and trousers of her uniform until they fitted her trim little figure.

Another member of our English section was an American Chinese, Ho Teh, who had been adopted by an American missionary family and spent her childhood in America. Her mannerisms and speech were typically American but in the end she had rejected her adoptive parents and returned to China. She, like me, had yearned to find her own family but in her case it was impossible. She had been picked up as a baby from the streets by a kind-hearted American couple. 'Somewhere among these millions,' she said to me once, 'I have relatives.' She would go off in a fantasy world dreaming of the kind of people they were likely to be. She had no child-hood memories to build her dreams upon but, like me, she needed her own identity. She had volunteered for service in Korea during the war and worked with American prisoners of war. 'The trouble with those Yanks,' she said in a typical American drawl, 'is that they've got no morale. Take away their vitamin pills and they turn their faces to the wall and die!'

She had never come into contact with any but middle-class Americans, having spent her time in the rarified atmosphere of a middle-class American home and a college campus.

'They're just a bunch of illiterates,' she exclaimed once. It had come as a shock and a revelation to find that the great American way of life, which she had been so enthusiastic about, had let her down in Korea and she was disillusioned with all things American. From being 100 per cent American she was now 100 per cent anti-American.

'There was this American lootenant who thought Lenin's "One Step Forward, Two Steps Back" was about ballroom dancing! Well, I ask you, how illiterate can they be!' she exclaimed in her drawl. She still found it easier to express some ideas in English.

119

Fifteen women from several sections of the radio station were to sleep in a room ten feet by seven, with a mud floor, tattered paper ceilings and torn paper windows. One girl had already been there several weeks; apparently she had some '*su hsiang wenti*' – minor ideological problems – and was there until she had straightened herself out through labour. Her '*sun hsiang wenti*' consisted of her husband discovering her in bed with his friend. She was too ashamed to speak to us and only answered when spoken to.

Our bedding rolls had been dumped by our male colleagues in a pile in the centre of the room. We looked at each other bewildered, wondering how we were going to place our quilts in a way that gave us all room to lie and sleep.

'I guess it's back to army discipline,' Ho Teh said, giving me a nudge. Her Korean experiences gave her that much superiority over the others.

'We'll just have to organize, goddamn it,' she said, and promptly disappeared to inspect the latrines.

I placed my quilt nearest the wall, gathered up some rice straw and pushed it under my quilt to give added warmth. Chang took her cue from me, and did the same. We looked at each other, shrugged our shoulders and moved Ho Teh's inflatable rubber mattress and quilt next to hers. There was not enough room to blow the mattress up as the next quilt overlapped. 'She will have to sleep on it flat,' I said to Chang as we pushed a smaller quantity of straw under. At night we lay in each other's laps as we slept; when one turned, we all had to turn, like a giant caterpillar slowly moving its hump along its body.

We got up at four in the morning, took our wash basins, went out into the dark cold yard and queued for water. None of us had slept well and our bodies ached from the hard floor.

Shivering with cold, Chang said to me in a whisper: 'Cheo Ying, I can't stand three weeks of this!'

She sat on a stool, while I went and queued for our breakfast. I was doled out some steaming hot millet porridge. It was like being in the army again and I looked forward to this 'labour reform'. I took a bowl back to Chang. 'What's this?' she exclaimed in horror, and backed away from it.

'It's millet,' I said, 'it's good and hot.'

'I thought only budgerigars ate millet.'

'Well, get that down you, you'll be eating horse-feed as well,' I answered unsympathetically.

We were ready by half past five to march in a column, army-style, to the reservoir site. We walked and stumbled over four miles of rugged trackless terrain, over rocks and hills. Not a tree or bush grew anywhere. Everything seemed dead and deserted. At the head of the column was the leader of our contingent, an ex-Armyman, now an official from the personnel department of the radio station. He had his long padded coat slung over his shoulders and strode forward, looking for all the world like a prototype Communist hero soldier of the films. He probably realized it. He had taken several groups of radio station personnel over the same track and was well seasoned.

We walked for two hours and got to the site just after seven. We threw ourselves down on the ground exhausted, hot and sweating. It had been ice cold when we set out. Now the sun had risen and was beating down on us. Our 'leader' stood in the centre and gave the orders. We were told to collect our spades and picks. They lay piled in an untidy heap. The spades had handles about five feet long and looked ungainly and I could not see how one used them efficiently. I rummaged around and found an ordinary garden spade, the metal part square shaped. I watched the others tentatively pick up the spades not quite knowing how to hold them. Some of the men bent to lift up the picks and seemed surprised at the weight – they staggered, not sure where best to hold the handle. We trooped off to our allotted sites. The men with the picks held them in various awkward positions. One man raised the pick over his head, staggered backwards with the weight, and fell into a trench, piercing his arm on the pick. He fainted and had to be carried off. Ho Teh, who turned up late after first, in typical American fashion, checking the 'sanitary arrangements', was given a basket and told to remove all insects and worms from the piles of newly dug earth. Insects, she was told, tunnelled holes in the dam and let the water out! In her eagerness to be the first to catch the worm, she caught her forehead on the end of someone's long-handled spade and

121

developed a pigeon-sized bump, and in the days that followed the bruise travelled from the bump to rest in the hollows of her eyes making her look like a prize panda. Before our three weeks were up, the colours had changed from black, to blue, to purple, to red, to yellow-green. Ignorance is bliss. She picked up all kinds of horrors and asked innocently as she dangled an angry scorpion by its hooked tail: 'Is this one an enemy?' Fortunately she was never stung or bitten.

An Irish navvy would have laughed himself silly at the spectacle of our feeble attempts at digging. Some stuck their spades into the ground, stood on them, and rocked backwards and forwards to push the spade deeper into the rock-hard earth, then jumping off and levering the clod. Several spades broke that way. Whoever designed them must have had a warped sense of humour and not liked intellectuals very much, because the handles towered above some of the diggers and made walking behind them a hazardous path.

Work stopped at ten for a fifteen-minute break. A man appeared with a pole across his shoulders carrying two wooden buckets of hot water. 'Hot water to drink! Hot water to drink!' he called out. We dashed forward with our mugs and were ladled hot water covered with a thick film of dust. I handed a mug to Chang: 'Here you are, salt-and-pepper water!' She took it wearily. We were too hot and parched to mind what was in the water. 'How can you joke, Cheo Ying? I won't be able to stand this!' and a tear collected the dust, leaving a white furrow down her cheek.

'Oh come,' I tried to laugh her out of despair. 'It's more fun than taking down my stutters on the radio. I prefer this, to reading a *People's Daily* editorial any day.'

As we sat and sipped our hot water, some of our group requested the help of 'our comrade workers' to show them how to use the tools properly. There had been too many accidents through ignorance and our quotas could not be set realistically if we were to go on losing people at the rate of that first morning.

Work stopped while some workers were sent from the actual dam to come to demonstrate how to use a pick and spade. Our group sat and the intent looks on their faces were as earnest as if they were watching a delicate piece of surgery.

This was for many of them the first time that they had actually looked closely at how manual work was done. My years in Dr Barnardo's and Staffordshire, where coal shovelling was a weekly chore, made me a survivor and I had no qualms of conscience when I sat on my spade and hid it, in case the workers took mine instead of those long-handled monsters. They did not appear to be too efficient with them, either. The shape and design were all wrong. The earth was hard-baked with the sun and one could not get enough pressure on the round-shaped tool to give a firm push. My square-shaped tool bit evenly into the hard earth and I was able to finish my allotted piece of ground and take time to look around me.

Each government organization had its own area to dig up. Next to ours was a group from the Foreign Ministry, including a couple of vice-premiers and the head of the Foreign Ministry Press Department, a hard-faced woman who terrified members of the foreign press. I wondered what they would think now if they saw her sweating, clad in a dirty mud-stained uniform. She was way behind her quota, and was criticized for chain-smoking. Someone had unkindly estimated the time wasted on 'lighting up' her cigarettes. There was also 'madame minister' from the Health Department, cheerfully shovelling away and covering people around her with flying earth. It was like standing behind a terrier digging for rabbits.

By the end of the day black-haired Chinese had become ash blondes. Our faces were thick with engrimed dust. Those who wore spectacles found it easier to take them off, and so with their perpetual squinting the creases lay white around their eyes, giving them a surprised look as if someone had suddenly kicked them.

The site from a distance looked as if it was covered with thousands of blue ants. Lines of swaying figures with baskets of earth suspended from a carrying pole across the shoulders meandered for nearly two miles to the dam. Unless one knew how to swing with a certain rhythm, thereby balancing the weight of the baskets, the pole could raise enormous red blisters on the top of the shoulders and behind the neck. Hundreds of others dug, picked out roots and insects before flinging the spadeful of earth into waiting baskets.

We were competing against the Foreign Ministry, the *People's Daily*, the Foreign Languages Press and a group from the Conservatory of Music. My hands had blistered, the blisters had broken and reblistered by the end of the day. I wondered how it affected the pianists and violinists until I noticed that as soon as the first blister appeared they stopped digging and took to picking up roots and insects instead.

At one p.m. we stopped for lunch: steaming baskets of maize pyramid loaves and salted turnip followed by the inevitable dusty hot water. Chang lay on the dry earth. Her delicate hands and polished nails, now cut and bleeding, covered her face, a picture of abject misery.

'Just let me rest,' she muttered, as I passed her a maize cake. I felt sorry for her and vowed that I would help dig her quota and make her 'labour reform' easier to bear. Chang had often made me cross in her criticisms of me at work, but unlike some I felt her points were fair and kindly meant, whereas Wei Ling and Mark Li's criticisms always made me feel suspicious and resentful, sending me off to Alan in a hateful rage.

The digging was not too difficult. It was no harder than removing the pile of coal regularly dumped in front of our 'entrance' in Staffordshire and carrying a bucket in each hand to the back coal-shed.

'Take it easy,' I said to Chang. 'I'll do yours, it's nothing with this spade,' and I made the earth fly, while she held hers at an almost horizontal angle with about three foot of pole behind her.

Now we lay like hundreds of others, too tired to move and hardly able to eat the dry maize and pickle.

Ho Teh passed us a toffee. 'It's good and meaty,' she said. Her American adoptive parents kept her well-supplied with food and still wrote loving letters which she so cheerfully took for granted. She was very conscious of calories and her outcry throughout our three weeks of labour was: 'But we are wasting calories this way!' She had a large supply of sweets, for 'energy' as she put it.

A group of girls came from a neighbouring opera troupe, sang songs and danced as we lay on the ground. The songs were about the glory of labour and the dances mimed digging, shovelling and carrying. The whole act was called 'Glory to the Ming Tomb Reservoir and to our great saviour Mao Tse-tung!' We clapped and cheered. I suppose it was meant to raise our flagging morale. But there is a limit to physical endurance. The limit was reached quickly by people who had until then lived only among books, papers and learning and were now suddenly flung into a situation the complete opposite of that to which they had been conditioned. They were puny, weak and undersized and the unaccustomed manual work taxed them beyond their limits. Even the luxury of being able to moan and complain over their pain and exhaustion was regarded as undesirable sentiment. The inevitable comment was made, 'But workers do this every day.' The misery and wretchedness had to be suppressed behind a false bravado of spurring each other on to higher and higher feats of endurance.

When we finishined at five and prepared for the long trek back to our quarters, Chang could hardly move. I supported her tottering steps as she placed one Clarkes crepe-soled walking shoe after another.

Chang and Ho Teh sat wearily on their bedding while I brought their basins of water and told them to wash their feet.

'I'm too goddamned tired,' Ho Teh snarled.

'Wash your feet, it doesn't matter about your face and hands,' I said. 'It will revive you.' I added slyly, looking at Ho Teh, 'It's an old army trick.'

I was revelling in my role. For once the situation was reversed. I was on the winning side and for three weeks I basked in the rays of their gratitude and good will. I knew that Chang, honest and gentle, would never again look at me with the same intellectual superiority when we returned to the radio station. I felt so virtuous and good that I could afford to be magnanimous and do their share of work and fetch their water and food. I grew tougher and stronger not only from the physical exercise and outdoor life but also from a self-enhancing glow from within. It proved one thing. My childhood in a Midland coal-miner's family had paid off and for the first time I looked back on that childhood with gratitude instead of regret.

There were many false entrances into the Ming Tombs and it was feared that priceless relics might be damaged if they were broken into at the wrong places. Engineers and archaeologists took painstaking care, even calling in the army with mine detectors. We occasionally dug up pottery and other relics which were taken to the main site to be examined and assessed.

Eventually the true entrances were found to the main burial chambers, opening up a treasure house of wealth and beauty. When the reservoir was finally finished, the tombs became a museum with the treasures restored and placed for everyone to see.

When I went back a couple of years later, acting as interpreter to a group of foreign visitors, the dust of Peking had lessened and blinding dust storms were getting rare. I saw a beautiful dam, a huge lake and trees all green and lush. I tried to work out what part we had dug, where that particular site might be. But there was nothing familiar to give me a clue. Looking at all that man-made beauty it was difficult to believe that I was ever there and I wondered if perhaps we were not digging for the reservoir at all but it was one big joke played upon us, because all our efforts meant nothing except as a lesson to ourselves, while the actual work of constructing the dam was really for the experts. I hoped not. It would be satisfying to feel that some of that beauty those foreign visitors were gazing at and admiring was made by me.

All I have to remind me of my reform through labour is a scar on my little finger where a razor-sharp edge of a spade nearly sliced it off, and a medal I was given for being a model worker.

10
Love – China Style

When I was four years old I was 'engaged' to a young son of a Chinese war-lord. The war-lord was a friend of my father and the two families decided to cement the friendship even closer by arranging a marriage between their children. The boy was a puny eight-year-old dressed in traditional long gown and a little black pimple hat. I pulled one of his protruding ears and made it bleed and then ran screaming to Ni Noo, my amah, accusing him of having kicked me. While our two nurses quarrelled, we peeped out behind their backs and pulled faces at each other.

After the revolution the old-fashioned way of parents arranging marriages for their children was regarded as reactionary, part of China's feudal past. Young couples were no longer required to obey their parents' choice of partners, but after centuries of custom it was not replaced by young people simply picking their own partners. The first law passed with the setting up of the New Republic was the marriage law. Girls were theoretically free to marry whom they pleased and men were allowed only one wife.

I was able to get a Peking divorce from Don, my first husband, which only required a letter from my office to say they approved of the divorce. He had eventually flown to Peking from Taiwan with a squadron of his former air-force friends bringing their American planes with them. They were welcomed as heroes and absorbed into the Red Air Force. Don wanted to pick up the threads of our marriage, but more than a year had passed since we parted in Hongkong and too much had happened for me to have any feelings left for him other than revulsion. I was still in love with Wang T'ao. The marriage law gave me the way out: I got a divorce on the grounds of '*Ssu Hsiang Pu T'ung*' – ideological differences. Wang T'ao's wife, a chairman of a state farm in Heilungkiang province still refused to give him a divorce although they rarely met except on festivals when she came down to Peking bringing their two sons to see him. I met her only once during a concert when he proudly showed me the boys. She stood there smiling, pretty and petite making me feel awkward and clumsy. I could not feel any animosity but refused to see Wang T'ao until she returned to the North-East.

In a house not far from my dormitory lived a property-owner who had four wives. His houses were confiscated and all he had left was the home he occupied with his wives and children. His source of income dried up and he became a worried man. He would have gladly welcomed his wives' taking advantage of their newly granted freedom, but as they had always got on well and loved their joint children, they had learned to live in harmony. They decided to form a sewing cooperative to keep the family together. They did very well, and their roles became reversed; the old man did the cooking and cleaning and the wives became the breadwinners.

Brothels closed down when the cities were taken over. Prostitutes, sing-song girls, beggars and homeless waifs were sent to be re-educated and trained for various skills. They were treated with compassion and understanding – as victims rather than criminals. Many of the young orphans were placed in peasants' homes and brought up as their own. Older children were sent to boarding schools. Prostitutes, rather fittingly, were trained as midwives and nurses. The incorrigibles were sent to work in factories, in small towns far away from the big cities and temptation. Opium smokers were cured by the drastic step of denying them all supplies of the drug. The state simply took control of all opium production at source. Street performers on the fringes of the semi-criminal classes were put into theatres left vacant by the strip-tease artists and their ilk. I saw them putting on their show in market places collecting a few cents one week and then the next in theatres performing to enthusiastic crowds and given grand titles such as 'Honoured State Artiste'. Later they travelled abroad delighting sophisticated audiences with their feats.

Public dance-halls and night clubs closed down. China became a nation of puritans. Sex life became difficult even in the confines of many marriages, but outside the marriage bond well nigh impossible.

The young men in my office were obsessed with the thought that they would never be able to get married and father children. A man's life is incomplete without issue, they would cry out in study groups.

One evening as we were quietly working at our desks, one young man suddenly stood up and screamed at his colleague across the room: 'I saw you! I saw you! Dipping that pen in the inkwell is a sign you want to make love to Yang Lo!' He was overpowered by Hsiang Li and Scoops and taken away. I looked astonished at the man he had accused. He was sitting there crying. I felt sorry for him but Hsiang Li and Scoops just looked at him in disgust. 'You're like a weak woman! If you want to develop a relationship with Yang Lo, then ask someone to make the necessary introduction.' And they went on with their work.

Scoops was accused of rape by a girl from the music conservatory when he refused to marry her. He denied the accusation and she was asked to prove her case. She produced a pen which she said he had given her the first time they went into the ricefield together. 'Well, how many times has he raped you?' asked Huang Chen gently. 'Many times, I've lost count,' she replied. Scoops had to make a self-criticism on his immoral behaviour and then ended up by volunteering for Korea to allow the scandal to die down. He was actually terrified that he might have to marry the girl. A husband was found for her eventually, the chairman of the local Young Communist League, who was in his fifties. He was too shy to find a wife or know what was required of him when he married. With typical Chinese thoroughness the Party considered it was a good match as she at least knew the ropes. It was a great relief for Scoops who said to us in the dormitory where we were giving him a farewell send-off the night he left for Korea, that he would rather have done one self-criticism a week for the rest of his life than marry that 'stupid Fatso'.

Sometimes a friend acted as a middleman in getting two

people together but that was a risk not many people were willing to take because the rules had changed. Whereas match-making used to be based on wealth and position, now a new yardstick was adopted: whether the potential partners' ideologies and political levels were compatible.

Sometimes the organization took on the role of the middle-man in choosing suitable husbands and wives. Many young and middle-aged men went to the Party branch to complain that they could not work properly, that efficiency was falling behind, and asked for help. In self-criticism meetings, the fear of not finding a 'companion for life' seemed to be the most cited reason for poor work, rather than lack of sexual experience which was regarded as characteristic of 'barb-arians'. When brother Hsiang Li thought it was time he got married, he went to his mother's village and found a pretty peasant girl. For her, he was a good catch – a government offi-cial from the capital of Peking. 'She's my Pygmalion;' he told me cheerfully, as I looked at the rather simple peasant girl and wondered what they had in common. It was Saturday night, and he turfed me out of my dormitory. I took my bedding roll and slept in Li Mei's empty bed. She had gone to spend the night with her lawyer husband, who lived in an organization on the other side of the city.

The women members of our group did not seem to be so preoccupied with sex and marriage. Marriage to them seemed to offer mainly the prospect of becoming mere child-bearing machines. In the evenings when we lay in our beds, we unwound and discussed problems of sex and love, and for the married ones different methods of birth control. They were on my side when I asked my organization to approve the divorce from Don, whereas the male members of my political study group were against divorcing him as 'he should be rewarded for bringing back so many pilots and planes'! The married women seemed to be used by their husbands 'like a lavatory', remarked one cynically. There was no attempt at making love in the sense of wanting to give pleasure. One was not sup-posed to enjoy it. In those early days, contraceptives were impossible to buy. Chairman Mao Tse-tung had stated that China's wealth lay in her people, which was interpreted as a patriotic duty for all wives to bear as many children as possible. And there would be tears as a woman once again found herself pregnant while the husband stood by mouthing comforting political clichés yet equally depressed at the prospect of nine months of a shrewish bitter wife. I wrote to 'Auntie' in England and asked her to send me some contraceptives, hastening to assure her they were for my friends. Soon I received ten thick rubber condoms which could be washed and used again. She called them 'working-men's washables'. I gave one to Li Mei, whose husband had claimed to her organization that his poor work was the result of her refusal to accept him on Saturday nights. She was advised 'for the sake of the work' to allow him to visit her. Even the satisfaction of motherhood was denied her, because as each baby was born she put it in a state nursery, where it lay swaddled with a score of other babies, in rows like silk-worm cocoons, to be picked up, fed, changed and put down again. Chinese babies are never 'burped'. For Li Mei and her husband, the work came first; there was no time for maternal care and love. They regarded both as sacrifices to the cause.

On Chinese New Year, I arranged the rest of the 'working-men's washables' on my desk, standing upright like a row of anaemic bananas, and invited the girls to receive their 'foreign' present. With screams of laughter we tried to blow one up like a balloon but despite beetroot faces from the effort the condom retained its original shape. I never heard of the results except from one who told me her scientist husband was using theirs to cover a glass experimental tube in the laboratory.

Sometimes a man, particularly if he held a responsible position, might approach a girl and suggest that he raise her political level. No mention was made of love. The courtship took the form of daily walks around the lanes of Peking or accompanying each other on office outings, and partnering at the occasional Saturday-night dance. The conversation was restricted to discussing the latest political event, or speeches, or problems relating to work. There was no talk of love.

Gradually people accepted that these two comrades were '*lien ai*' (making a love alliance). The man then consulted some responsible comrades and asked for their advice regarding marriage. Only if the answer was positive did he propose.

The same arrangements were made on the girl's side. Comrades then approached the couple and discussed whether marriage benefited them politically and in their work. A simple reception was held, with cups of green tea, melon seeds and a plate of biscuits; a leading comrade was invited to make a speech and toast the future happiness of the couple. The speech invariably urged them to make a better contribution to the Communist cause and wished them many children to help build a strong, powerful, new China. Speech ended, they were regarded as married. In those early days there was no formal wedding ceremony or marriage certificate.

The most lively part of the day was in the evening before the couple retired to the bridal chamber suitably decorated with flowers, a silk coverlet on the marriage bed which was simply two single beds pushed together. Red was the predominant colour and huge portraits of Marx, Engels, Lenin and Stalin gazed down on the nuptial couple. Often the room was one of the smaller dormitories where the other single people moved out for the night to squeeze into other rooms so that the newly weds could spend their first night together. Before retiring to the room, they had to suffer the teazing and tricks of their friends, a custom called '*Nao Shin Fang*' (creating havoc in the bridal chamber). Assorted objects were put in the bed – a baby's bottle, a doll, thistles between the quilts, alarm clocks hidden in different parts of the room and set to go off at all hours of the night. Finally when everyone was tired of the japes, the couple were allowed to retire. From then on, the pair joined the Saturday-night manoeuvres. At that time, in the early fifties, people were still billeted in single-sex dormitories. A few lucky couples had a room of their own, but in the main, girls cooperated by sharing bunks on Saturday nights and leaving odd smaller rooms for husbands to pay a marital visit. Sometimes on hot humid nights we single ones sat around in the courtyard, smoking, drinking tea and cracking melon seeds chatting the night away, while Hsiang Li who was a dab hand at 'foreign' cooking emerged with a lemon-meringue pie, which he had baked on top of a charcoal stove with a pot over it. The meringue was sticky and flat, and the pastry grey and doughy but they were harmonious warm nights, full of comradeship and quiet happiness. For a brief spell we could forget our next self-criticism, political reports and the dread of another campaign.

Saturday nights, after work, the showers were packed with eager husbands and wives getting cleaned up for their weekly night together. On Sunday mornings they collected their children from the nursery, cooked a meal together and spent this one day a week living as a family. Sunday was a happy relaxed day. No one felt at that time that life should be any different from this spartan régime because as government cadres one sacrificed one's own comforts for the cause of Communism. In the evening the children returned to the nursery and the parents separated until the following Saturday. If a campaign was under way or some serious political discussion going on, then even this night was cancelled. An ambitious young couple could always depend on praise for their revolutionary fervour if they stayed on at their places of work rather than be together. It was considered a good test.

A couple of months after I arrived at the Hsinhua News Agency, Hu Hsi, a young editor on the *People's Daily* came to me one day and said: 'Comrade Cheo Ying, your political level is low, I would like to help you.' I took him at his word. I had already made a public self-examination regarding Wang T'ao, and my morale was low. It seemed that with my western bourgeois background I needed all the help I could get, so I welcomed his suggestion. He was quite tall with long teeth like a horse. 'You can call me "The Lone Wolf",' he said one day quite seriously and I smiled and wondered whether I dared tell him what the other meaning was in English, but I did not think he would see the point. He was much too serious and had no sense of humour. Most likely he would criticize me for flippancy.

We met every evening and wandered round the building, or sat together in the canteen talking politics. He questioned me on my background, my attitudes to work and study and at the same time slipped in details of his own background, letting me know what a brave soldier he had been in the Liberation Army. 'See this scar here?' and he rolled up a trouser leg and exposed a thick calf with a knotted white scar. 'That was a Japanese bayonet.' If I felt he was a little immodest it was quelled by the thought that a man in his position behaved like

133

that because it was all true. I considered him a very brave man and felt flattered that he should want to help me with my studies and improve my political understanding.

A few weeks later I was called to the personnel office where several people I knew awaited me including Wei Ling, Huang Chen and Li Mei. They looked very severe. Huang Chen asked me what my motives were in relation to Hu Hsi, who had asked their permission to marry me! I gaped in astonishment and before I could answer, Huang Chen said, 'Of course we cannot agree to this match. There is still the matter with Comrade Wang T'ao. Does he know of this?' I was asked if I had anything further to say about Wang T'ao apart from what I had already admitted in group meetings. They knew that we were just marking time before a change took place in his own situation. But until I specifically said so, they were content to let sleeping dogs lie. Wang T'ao as a high-ranking officer still had overall responsibility for me because he had placed me there. It was obvious that Huang Chen wanted to know what the real situation was before taking any action. Occasionally Wang T'ao and I had met and walked in Pei Hai Park but avoided any references to our past relationship. It was as if that chapter of our lives was temporarily closed. Only once when skating on the frozen lake I slipped and fell, he ran and pulled me up and held me close for a brief moment before letting me go again.

Huang Chen and Li Mei were concerned that I should be 'encouraging' Hu Hsi and at the same time not relinquishing my contacts with Wang T'ao while Wei Ling said snappishly: 'You are displaying a flippant attitude towards personal relations. Remove this romanticism from your soul. Hu Hsi is young and is being groomed for a responsible position. It would jeopardize his future if he has to spend time helping you to solve your ideological problems!'

'If he had asked me first, I would have said no, anyway,' I snapped and walked out of the room without another word.

Back in the dormitory, furious and ashamed, I lay on my bunk and began squashing the bed bugs on the wall saying: 'Take that! and that! and that!' I had been made to feel as if I was the hunter and he the victim. A shadow fell over my bed. I turned my head, my bloody finger raised in the process of squashing another bug, and saw Hu Hsi standing there. He was white-faced and trembling.

'What do *you* want?' I asked rudely.

He replied: 'I want to talk to you. I have spoken to the Party about us and they have said to choose between you and the Party. I am willing to take that risk, if you will marry me.'

'I never want to see you again,' I said, turned my back on him and managed to squash a fat bug before it disappeared into a crack behind the light socket. After a few seconds the shadow disappeared and when I looked he had gone.

I was helping Hsiang Li and his wife re-quilt their bedspread. He had cleared out a tiny cubby hole by the porter's gate with the only light and air coming through the latticework door. His wife and I had lime-washed the walls and patched up the holes in the paper ceiling. Hsiang Li had made his single bed into a double by just fitting in extra planks and it could just fit in the tiny room with enough space for a small table. By day we could sit on the bed and use it as a kind of platform, with the bedding and clothes rolled up in neat bundles and placed lengthways like cushions against the damp wall. Now we were unstitching their single quilts and turning them into a double one.

I was depressed. Wang T'ao had flown to the North-East to visit his wife who had complained to the Party of his neglect. I felt I was being manoeuvred into a position from which I could not extricate myself and yet did not have the courage to tell him. I tried to lessen the frequency of our meetings and was relieved when he went off for several months at a time to the North-West province of Sinkiang supervising the construction of nuclear energy sites. Then as the months went by I began to miss him and wonder so that when he returned and I heard his voice on the telephone asking whether I had been good and working hard and whether I had missed him, I felt relief again that he still cared. There was still strong affection for him and I alternated between wishing he would return to his wife permanently and hating her for being the obstacle.

'It's all very well for you,' I moaned to Hsiang Li. 'Nobody takes me seriously except when Wei Ling has to go to the sanatorium and there is no one else to do the work. She keeps bringing up Hu Hsi at every group meeting we have. I did not encourage him.' The lime had made my eyes sore and red and a few tears fell on the quilt.

Hsiang Li said: 'The trouble with you is that you're too '*li hai*' (fiery) and offered to find me a young peasant from his village. Two years earlier I might have seriously considered it but I was beginning to realize that I could no longer suppress the influences of my English childhood. At times it was as if there were two beings, one Chinese, one English, fighting all the time to come out on top. I was just a confused person who was neither one thing or another. The English and American proof-readers around me were reinforcing the European influences within me. Sometimes I resented them and wished they would go away so that I would not have the chance of making comparisons and therefore accept the life I had chosen.

By then, there were many foreigners, some in the diplomatic missions, trade delegations and those who had been invited to come to China to train technicians and as advisers. We had to take turns in interpreting and accompanying these foreigners on unofficial outings. I enjoyed the occasional break from official routine but even this was frowned on if I went outside my terms of reference and accompanied individuals to the International Club. The relevant embassy was told that a certain member of its staff had been seen in the company of a Chinese cadre and a polite diplomatic hint was dropped. A report was sent to my office and temporarily I would be taken off the list of interpreters and be hauled over the coals for exceeding my terms of reference. Standing up in front of the group I criticized myself and promised to do better in future, ending up with the pious hope that my comrades would help me reform. I had learnt to become a political hypocrite. Wei Ling actually smiled on me and omitted to put me on a thirty-six-hour shift. My conscience would prick and sometimes I wished I could openly express my true thoughts and speak out about the the problems and frustrations. Why couldn't a man come up to me and say, 'I love you, I desire you,' instead of saying, 'Let me raise your political level'? I hated the hypocritical two-faced atmosphere and when I could not longer restrain my thoughts I would storm off to Alan's flat to let off steam. He laughed at me: 'Why can't you accept you're a bloody non-conformist and a rebel?'

Hsinhua was like my family and I did rebel against the petty restrictions it made. Sometimes I sneaked off and went dancing at the International Club, using Alan as my alibi. It was supposed to be reserved for the foreign diplomatic community and was placed under the eagle eye of the Chinese Foreign Ministry, barring all Chinese girls. Like Cinderella before the last dance, I had to dash off before someone tried to see me home. Taking off my dress, I changed back to my uniform and returned to my dormitory. A romantic Pole discovered where I lived and hovered outside my dormitory leaving flowers and chocolates with an embarrassed guard at the gate. Then a Bulgarian zoomed up in a flashy Volkswagen and asked for 'that pretty half-Chinese girl'. Each time Huang Chen wearily sent for me and said: 'Not again, Comrade Cheo Ying!' and suggested I marry Hsu Ming, a roly-poly little man with a nose like a snout. He was considered an ideal match for me. But I did not want to have a serious relationship with anyone, not while I still felt tied to Wang T'ao.

I was twenty, bored and still single. All my dormitory mates had married and the only one left in the room was Chen Ming-t'ao, whose husband, after solidly banging at the gate every Saturday night for almost a year to get at his wife and consummate the marriage, was now starting divorce proceedings. She still scratched at her allergic rash and sometimes I sat on my bed, my head on my knees and cried out in sheer frustration: 'What a goddamned life!' Hsiang Li's wife was expecting their first baby and he was very happy. Scoops was in Korea working with American POWs. Wei Ling was in a sanatorium with TB, and I found myself missing the daily spice of our mutual antagonism. My life seemed to be one boring round of broadcasting turgid *People's Daily* articles cliché-ridden until I could practically read them off by heart, then back to reports, study sessions, criticism and self-criticism meetings and so to my dormitory and itchy Chen Ming-t'ao. Once in a temper I told her go and see the doctor and she replied: 'I'm not letting any man touch me!'

One day I was at the radio station trying to unwind yards of recording wire which had spun off the machine and become a tangled mess, when a group of foreign technicians came round on a tour of the broadcasting studios. Among them was a blond Czech. To me he seemed like a Greek God, and I decided there and then that he was the man I wanted. Karel said afterwards that when he saw me crawling around the floor entangled in yards of silver wire, cursing, it was the first natural thing he had seen in the otherwise artificaly perfect atmosphere of the radio station.

He knelt down and helped unravel the recording wire. I saw a flash of multi-coloured striped socks which seemed incongruous with his formal baggy Russian-style suit. He spoke English, ending his sentences on an upward lilt so that at first I did not know whether he was going to say more. In that enclosed space of the recording studio I could smell his sweat and after the scentlessness of Don and Wang T'ao I did not mind it. A signal light went on from the broadcasting studio. Wei Ling, refreshed after her hospital stay, had finished a long *People's Daily* tirade against American imperialism and I had to hurry in and put on a record of Paul Robeson. Karel watched from behind the glass screen. In my confusion I switched on the wrong speed and instead of the deep bass tones of Paul Robeson a sound like a squeaking mouse came over the air. I gave an agonized look at Wei Ling, who glared at me, and then I saw Karel roaring with laughter. I felt a bubble begin to rise in my throat and my eyes streamed with tears as I fought hard to keep from laughing out loud. I switched over to the mike and announced in solemn tones, 'That was Paul Robeson, the great American Negro Peace fighter singing "Old Man River".' I switched off and collapsed in uncontrollable laughter. 'I'm sorry Wei Ling, I'm sorry,' I gasped. 'It was his fault,' nodding towards Karel. She was so angry she could not speak but walked away. If she could have smiled just a little I would have made a sincere self-examination at the inevitable group meeting, but the contrast between Karel's reaction and hers only made his laughing face appear over and over again in my mind as Wei Ling bumbled on and on and I heard the words "flippancy," "low political level," "backward thinking" as a minor accompaniment. It made me turn to him as a thankful alternative to the utter seriousness of life at the radio station.

I loved him so much that it hurt. To think of him during political group discussions, his passion for multi-coloured striped socks, his golden hair, brought tears to my eyes and made whoever was speaking stop and stare wondering what was the matter with me. Love for Wang T'ao seemed so meaningless and shallow and the past two years of uncertainty did not create a strong enough basis without physical love to keep the relationship going. Karel could love away my inhibitions and fears until I felt my whole tight self-control unfreeze in a warm enhancing glow. He had leukemia and I tried to kiss away the festering sores that developed every time he received a graze or tiny cut, which he frantically burnt away with a tarry ointment. I pushed away the thought that the disease was terminal. We lived for the present, savouring the sheer delight of just being together. China, Czechoslovakia, politics, the whole gulf between our two worlds did not matter. When he first told me about his illness it was done in a casual, almost light-hearted, manner because he had learned to accept that he should live his life from day to day and not to think too far ahead and I assumed the same kind of attitude. We had walked from the east gate of Peking to the west gate, where I lived, one Siberian winter night discussing the implications that his illness would have on our future. I could sense in his attempts to be 'sensible about my short life' that there was a plea not to reject him. The numbness that went through my body helped to dreaden the dreadful cold of that winter night and when I sneaked into my dormitory in the early hours I realized I was clad only in a thin cotton uniform and then my body began to shiver and ache with cold. I got into bed and found that my room-mates had removed some of the planks from my bed as a joke. I sank through the gap, by then too weak to move, and lay there uncontrollably shivering until it was time to get up.

Karel's home town sounded just like an industrial town of the Midlands and in my mind's eye I could imagine the kind of life that marrying him would await me there, not dissimilar from any ordinary couple's life in the Midlands – the prospect from which I had run away. Now, with Karel, it seemed a wonderful contrast to the organizational life – the radio station, bad-tempered Wei Ling. I had shut my mind away from the depressing aspects of a small Czech town and shut my mind from the caring atmosphere of my life in the organization, of brother Hsiang Li, Huang Chen, Li Mei – my family. In my waking moments my mind was only on Karel and I marvelled at this new experience of loving someone so deeply for the first time in my life.

We decided to get in touch with our respective organizations and tell them of our intention to marry. We expected difficulties but there had been rare cases of Chinese girls marrying foreigners, especially during the short period of relaxation in 1951. I expected a few hysterical outbursts but thought as long as I insisted and showed that I did not care about leaving the revolutionary movement which was mandatory if a cadre married a foreigner, we could eventually get permission. This time Wang T'ao's worried words about a good Marxist finding a way made sense to me. He was a thousand miles away in the North-West and was just a shadow looming darker when I thought of what he would feel and do when he found out. But it was not so much Marxism as determination. I just needed to change the jargon. I had been open about my relationship with Karel right from the beginning and Huang Chen with a kindly smile on his Jerry Cruncher face listened while I raved and talked about my '*ching ai de*' (dearly beloved). I think he gained some kind of pleasure from my happiness as an antidote to his own miserable marriage, and so when I made a formal request for permission to marry Karel, Huang Chen relayed the answer: 'Yes, if the Czechs agree, we will agree.'

There seemed to be no obstacles. Karel wrote to his parents and they began to make preparations to meet their future Chinese daughter-in-law. Then the blow fell. A report was sent to the Czech Embassy which was calculated to leave them no alternative but to forbid any further contact between Karel and myself.

He managed to get a copy of the report and show it to me. 'Daughter of an American spy, former wife of a Kuomintang airman, flippant and flirtatious. . . .' Huang Chen denied that the report had come from him and I could only guess that he had passed on the responsibility of making it to a higher authority. Wang T'ao, I knew, had suddenly arrived back in

Peking, two weeks earlier but I had refused to see him because I was too preoccupied with my love for Karel to have any room left for him. I was also afraid to see him in case he used all the emotional and political pressure he was capable of and twisted me around. Once before, when I had left the Army to join the radio station, he had cried and the shock of seeing a man so powerful in tears had fed my vanity as well as weakened my resolve not to see him again. There were no extenuating circumstances in the report which could have given a more balanced picture. Nothing about my father being a stranger to me; nothing about the reasons for divorcing Don and nothing about Wang T'ao.

I ran all the way to his headquarters in the old Tartar City, pushed the guards aside and burst into his room. He knew I would come and there was a look of triumph on his face as I went on my knees, grasped his legs and begged him to retract the report. In the vague mists of despair I heard him trying to comfort me, kissing my tear-filled eyes, saying: 'We knew best, you are still very young – you would be all alone in a strange country – we would be unable to help you.' He murmured: 'Even if I did not love you the answer would be the same. This won't last, it is just an infatuation.'

In a frenzy I screamed out: 'What do you know about love?' and I slipped into the coarse language of the army: 'Whenever you feel like it you fly off to the North-East and fuck your wife and you leave me with fine words and promises!' He slapped me across the face so hard that it took my breath away and I lay on the floor crying. He lifted me and cradled me in his arms, kissing my face repeating over and over again, '*Wo ai ni, wo ai ni*' (I love you, I love you). My face was aching and I could feel the raised imprints of his long fingers on my cheek. I was calm and did not resist when he made love to me.

'I shall never see you again, Wang T'ao,' I said sadly. 'Even if you were free tomorrow, I will never see you again.' He smiled and stroked my face. 'You will, *ch'ing ai de*, when he's gone. I can see the future more clearly than you can.'

I hated him for his superior confidence and shook my head.

Karel and I appealed to the Czech Ambassador. But he was having troubles of his own. Our problem was minute

compared to the tense atmosphere that the Slansky trials in
1952–3 in Prague were causing all Czechs in embassies
abroad. Slansky was executed as a traitor and the government
was now investigating its embassies abroad for possible
Slansky sympathizers. The Czechs in Peking pounced on
Karel and me as a political gift to take the pressure off themselves. The ambassador and his staff busied themselves in
making the Cheo Ying–Karel question bigger than the
Slansky affair itself. There was no hope. Karel was ordered
back to Prague by the first available plane. He asked to be
allowed a final meeting with me and he stayed the night in the
empty dormitory. We were white and tense and the strain of
the past few weeks showed in the little festering sores on his
pasty face which he had not bothered to treat. I tried to be
happy for both our sakes. 'Your face looks like one of Hsiang
Li's meringue pies,' I said jokingly and then we sat on my
hard bed and sobbed in each other's arms. I kissed his poor
hands over and over again in an agony of grief and then knelt
on the floor and buried my head in his lap. 'You can't leave
me with nothing. I can't stop loving when you have gone.' It
was a night which I shall never want to live through again.

I begged tablets from doctor friends to drug myself into
sleep so as to get a brief respite from the thoughts and despair
at losing Karel. I awoke half stupefied; for a few seconds I lay
and wondered why there was such a tight pain inside my
chest. Then the thoughts and the sense of a great loss came
crowding in and I started crying all over again.

From Czechoslovakia Karel wrote that there was no
problem about our marriage, everything had been sorted out.
He said a visa was waiting for me. 'They can't stop us marrying here,' he wrote. But I knew the Chinese authorities would
never back down and let me go. It would have been a terrible
loss of face. I could not understand why, like other political
undesirables, I was still in a government organization as a
cadre doing important work if this was going to be the kind of
dossier that would appear on my file. What was wrong with
two young people wanting to marry? I wondered how much
Wang T'ao's influence had been brought to bear on the whole
attitude towards me in the radio station. My mind was then
too confused to sort out anything so complicated or to reason

how my actions affected him. Huang Chen, in trying to guide me out of my bewilderment, said in a kindly way: 'You don't want to marry a foreigner. They stink when they sweat, how could you bear it?' As for the report, everyone had shadows in their past and to prove there was no political discrimination regarding *Chinese* men, he would jump at the chance. It was made plain that even if I did apply officially to join Karel in Prague the Chinese authorities would turn it down.

In moments of clarity, I thought the Chinese had more important things to concern themselves with than the marriage plans of just one of their nearly 800 million nationals. But it was a classic example of how officials can be hysterical over petty things and keep their calm on bigger issues. A Foreign Ministry official recounted with great glee, as a lesson to us all, how one Chinese girl who had married a Hungarian before they could stop it was now desperately unhappy and wanted to return to China. 'But we won't let her,' commented one vice-premier smirking. 'What is wrong with our own Chinese men?'

I could see no future. I worked like an automaton, took my scripts, read them over the air, sat silent in meetings and hardly spoke. I could feel myself slowly freezing up and longed for time to help dull the yearning for Karel. It was so monstrous to deprive us of the few years he had left and I could feel myself slowly turning within myself, locking away my emotions and becoming once again that frozen Staffordshire child, punctuated every now and then by a burning hatred so strong against Wang T'ao that I felt I could take a gun and blow his superior head off – just as I had done to my dog Hsiao Mee. Wei Ling, Mark Li, Chang Ching-nien, always my severest critics, left me alone in my misery because I agreed with all their criticisms and hoped that they could work up enough political fodder to have me punished and sent away. But Huang Chen stepped in and told them to leave me alone. They turned their fire on Ho Teh instead using the same criticisms as on me because she was an American Chinese and had lots of bourgeois habits to overcome. I felt the millstone of my father's alleged crime hanging round my neck like the Ancient Mariner's albatross. Was that going to shadow the rest of my life? Sometimes in the brief moments of awareness I would shout out in a meeting: 'What am I doing here?' and wish I could bury myself and my grief in the depths of a Midland town, the very opposite of Peking.

Hsi Ming, a former suitor, hurriedly came back from Korea where he had been on the negotiating team for the armistice talks. He was my round, tubby little admirer from the Foreign Ministry, whom I had met during an interpreting job. Huang Chen asked him to try again. 'Perhaps Cheo Ying has seen sense, she needs an older person to keep her in line.' We went to the cinema, he daringly held my hand. I let him and watched the film. He proposed but did not press his suit when I said in English: 'If you like, but you'd better ask Wang T'ao.' He went back to Korea to continue negotiating. He may have found that job easier.

Sometimes I went to Sammy and his wife's home. They felt sorry and fussed over me. Sammy in his fumbling awkward way tried to cheer me up. 'Everyone has a lost love. That's life. Anyway, look what you've caused! You've made heads roll in Czechoslovakia over this Slansky affair. Not many young girls can beat that.' He made me laugh until the tears rolled down my face. Karel, in revenge for the part the embassy had played in our separation, had denounced them in Prague and they had one by one been recalled to face political banishment.

Alan came back from Korea for a few days and I turned to him for comfort. He made me feel safe and in the calmness that followed I said: 'Marry me, Alan.' It was not a serious proposal but I felt I needed someone to help me put a wall around my emotions so that they could never get hurt again. In some distorted way I thought I was getting my revenge on all those who had played a part in my heartbreak.

The day before he left for Korea again, we were sitting at a roadside stall eating a bowl of sheep's innards in a fiery sauce and washing it down with cups of white spirit made from millet. As we chatted we found ourselves talking about what we would do when we married. He was over twenty years older than I and there was no talk of love. I did not want it any more but it seemed a good way out for both of us. He had also suffered an unhappy experience but in his case the girl had killed herself. We were like two pieces of flotsam floating on a wave of Chinese hypocrisy and political machination. He wrote a formal application to the radio station before he left for Korea that night while I returned to the dormitory and wondered what people would say now, so soon after Karel.

A few days later, the request I had made earlier for a spell of labour reform during my troubles over Karel was granted. Whether it was their answer to Alan's request or not I never discovered. I was sent to a state farm near the North-East coast. The harvesting of maize was in full swing. I welcomed the physical work and actually enjoyed the change.

The food and conditions were only slightly worse than my early days in the army and I was not so affected as my fellow workers, who had joined government organizations in a spirit of national enthusiasm and then found they were unable to cope with the restrictions placed on their social and moral behaviour. A general's young wife had committed adultery with his bodyguard and spent most of the time weeping at the thought she would never see her children again. Another wife of a party secretary had been caught stealing baby clothes, and in the next bed to me was a beautiful young girl from the Foreign Ministry whom I nick-named 'The Startled Fawn'. She had had an affair with a Vietnamese diplomat which had not been discovered because he used to meet her dressed in the blue cotton uniform worn by all government cadres and was indistinguishable from other Chinese. She was five months pregnant before their affair was discovered. He was recalled while she was given an abortion. It was performed without proper anaesthetic and she was still bleeding several months later. Sometimes she screamed in her sleep, which woke us all with a start and we listened to her whimpering for the rest of the night. There was no comfort we could give.

The bad diet and poor conditions interrupted women's normal menstrual cycles so I was not unduly worried when mine did not arrive. I began to feel sick in the morning and to feel constant nausea during the day. We all suffered digestive ailments because of the bad diet. Dysentery was so common that we chewed raw garlic and red hot chilis to combat infection.

I was glad I was pregnant and I grew to love the first stirrings of life inside me and at night I hugged myself in delight at my secret. It belonged to me, to love without any restrictions. It was easy to hide my thickening waist-line under the bulky shapeless uniforms. There was no news from Alan and in letters to and from the radio station no mention was made on either side about his request. In the meantime I lived through those months in the hope that the nearer the time for my baby's birth the better chance of them being forced to accept a *fait accompli*.

One evening we were playing volley ball and a particularly hard shot hit me in the stomach. I clutched my nearly eight months weight and fell to the ground writhing in agony.

Wei Ling came to see me in hospital and brought a box of sweets. She sat silent while I greedily ate through the box. We had taken a peep at my yellow jaundiced little son and I knew she was longing to ask me who his father was but I wanted her to squirm. At last I finished the last of the sweets, wet my finger and licked up the bits of sugar which remained in the box and waited for her to speak. I had taken up a stance of defiance and triumph to make up for the dreadful ordeal I had gone through during the past months and I wanted her to suffer to make her realize that I could have the man she wanted and have babies she could not have. I would have gone on goading and gloating but she got up and crept out of the room. Tears started up in my eyes and I called her name but she did not turn back and I knew that I had lost the chance of ever making friends.

I brought my baby home in the news agency compound to a welcoming Huang Chen, Li Mei and Hsiang Li. They had prepared a tiny room off the main dormitories – a former stable for the imperial elephants and next to my hard plank bed a bamboo cradle. No questions were asked when they picked the baby up in turn and I looked on happy as Huang Chen cradled him and walked him up and down the tiny room. All my anger was overcome by a warm spread of love for them all. They were, after all, my family.

Several weeks later, as I came down from the steps of the radio station, there stood a car with Huang Chen and Li Mei, grinning all over their faces.

'Get in,' they said.

'Where are we going?' I asked.

'Wait and see,' was the reply.

The car sped towards the airport and they still said nothing but just sat there grinning. My heart gave a leap, not daring to hope. When we arrived a plane was coming in to land. Out stepped Alan. That was the first sign that they had approved my marriage to a foreigner. We could only look at each other and laugh. Alan said: 'Blimey, they don't give a man much time to change his mind.' We were bundled into the car which sped back to Peking. Then to the local register office, where we stood before a woman official. She spoke, but neither of us heard a word, our minds were in a whirl. Huang Chen said, 'Sign here.' We signed, the woman official shook our hands. We were married.

Back in the car Huang Chen chuckled: 'Well now to the jollities. We're having a party tonight in the office to celebrate. Everyone will be there. The Minister will give the main speech.

It was good to see smiling faces again. I felt as if a great cloud had been lifted and I was eager to please, to promise to work harder and better in gratitude. Huang Chen, his dear ugly face glistening with sweat, slightly drunk, said: 'You're much too "*li hai*" (fiery) for us. You can wear each other out.' Li Mei had taken little Joe into a small room off the hall and I heard him cry for his feed. I gave my glass to Alan and quietly disappeared. As I sat there and fed him I thought of the security that marrying Alan had given us and I was grateful. Even if Karel had walked through the door my exhilaration was such at that moment I would have spurned him. Suddenly I heard a voice shout out: 'Where is the bride? The Minister wants to toast the new bride!' and Huang Chen's tipsy reply: 'The bride's feeding the baby!'

They had hung huge silk embroidered pictures of Marx, Engels, Lenin and Stalin surrounding a bigger picture of Mao Tse-tung facing the bed. There were no alarm clocks under the bed, or thistles between the sheets. Neither was there a baby doll. There was a real one sleeping in the bamboo cradle at the foot of the bed.

Alan looked up at the disapproving expressions of the pictures: 'They can come down for a start,' he said.

11
Conflicts

Hsiang Li's wife Mei-hua and I were making wet coal balls out of left-over coal dust one morning when an embassy invitation was delivered addressed to me as 'Madam'. 'It's a good job they can't see what "madam" is doing at the moment,' I said to her, and we giggled like a couple of schoolgirls.

Soon after we married, Alan left for Korea again, covering the long-drawn-out armistice talks. He expected to be gone for a few days but the days dragged on for months. I saw no sense in moving into his flat and stayed in the dormitory to be nearer work. It was easy to live like a normal Chinese cadre with Alan out of sight but I wondered how things would be when he came back. I was beginning to have doubts about the idea that I was simply a Chinese, the notion which had motivated my whole life till then. But you do not suddenly become a different personality because of a piece of paper. Self-awareness creeps up on you insidiously and for a time you are in a state of flux where you make decisions and interpretations from a Chinese point of view and then in another situation your reactions are totally English. Making coal balls with Mei-hua, looking after her invalid mother when she and Hsiang Li went off for a spell of labour in the North-West, came as naturally as if she was my own mother. Hsiang Li and Mei-hua I loved as my own brother and sister. But then the flashes of temper as we argued from different points of view were not the reactions of a Chinese. During a criticism meeting after the sparrow campaign, I was asked to explain my motives in not taking part. It was customary for a meeting to start off with a person's good points being listed before actually criticizing their faults. In the end it became a time-wasting pattern but unless criticism balanced the good and the bad points it was not considered constructive. I knew when I had refused to kill the birds that I would have to explain and make a self-criticism. So when Wei Ling opened the meeting with the words: 'Comrade Cheo Ying's broadcast of yesterdays *People's Daily* editorial was excellent,' I groaned out loud: 'Here it comes!' 'That is the wrong attitude to take, comrade,' snapped Mark Li.

'You're just a bunch of hypocrites,' I yelled. 'Why don't you be open and frank and say what you really mean? It is such a waste of time.' That opened up a torrent of criticism of my contemptous attitude towards the masses.

I had sent a cable to Alan in Korea which said. 'In the pudding club again.' The cable was censored. Wei Ling demanded to know what it meant, accusing me of telling him something in code which I did not want the office to know. Since my marriage she had been the main instigator in reminding the organization that I should be transferred to the press department of the Foreign Minstry because of my foreign husband, in line with general policy. Greenbaum had also added his comment that foreigners should not have an easy way of getting unofficial news hand-outs. I had not moved into Alan's flat but still lived in the little cell-like room that Huang Chen had organized for me when I returned from the hospital. My comrades had brightened the room and delivered live chickens 'to bring on the milk'. Wei Ling had come to have a peep at 'the little mushroom' as she called him and I let her take him in her arms and hold him for a while. Her face softened and even looked beautiful. I felt ashamed of the ill-will I had felt towards her and trying to make amends I told her what 'pudding club' meant. 'I know,' she answered happily. 'Sammy told us.' A few moments later she spoilt the spirit of forgiveness by suggesting I should put little Joe in the office nursery so that my work would not be adversely affected. I grabbed the baby and pushed her out of the room. It was dark and silent except for the clucking of the chickens in the bamboo basket. I felt horribly frightened and alone. I could not bear to see my son swaddled like a cocoon in a row. Who would pick him up when he cried? I wanted to love and hold him, to let the waves of tenderness flow into his little body from mine. The thought of parting with him even temporarily was unbearable. I did not want him to grow up institutionalized like Li Mei's children – dull, unimaginative like automatons. If Alan had been there I might have felt differently but as yet he was not a real part of my life and was miles away in Korea. I had gone through the months of pregnancy, had the baby alone in the hospital and not thought that he should have been with me. When one has known a person as a friend for so long it takes time to be reconciled to the fact that he was now an important part of your life. I was fiercely protective over the baby, he was mine and mine only. I remembered the bitch I saw in that dog's Belsen years before who fought to protect her puppies from hungry dogs but looked appealingly at the policeman as he picked up one of them and dashed its brains out. She knew when the odds were too great. I sat and hugged Joe so hard he cried out. If this was what being a 'revolutionary mother' meant in Chang Ching-nien's terms then I wanted no part of it, and I craved for the security that Alan's presence might give.

As I sat through the night rocking the baby and myself to and fro, I thought of my old nurse, Ni Noo. I had heard that she had left my father's family after his arrest and was working in a garment factory in Shanghai. I knew instinctively that she would help me. It did not occur to me that she might not come. She had nursed me as a child; now she must nurse and care for my baby. I felt relieved and happy. Ni Noo would come.

In the morning I sent a cable to Shanghai and moved into Alan's flat. I cleared out the bits and pieces from my dormitory I had collected over the years which were precious to me: a piece of Hsiao Mee's fur, a picture of Lenin from Wang T'ao, my old music box, my wash basin and bedding. As I looked at the dormitory I knew I was saying goodbye to a standard of life I had got used to and accepted but was now giving up because I could not bear the same for my son. I was doing what we had all sneered at Sammy's wife Su Lan, for, when she moved into his flat with all its attendant comforts. I would miss Hsiang Li's soggy pies and the hardship which was not unpleasant because it was shared with people for whom I had deep affection. I piled my possessions on to a pedi-cab. Alan's home was miles away near the Pei Hai Park where I used to meet Wang T'ao. Living there would be more than just those miles removed from the dormitory life; it would be another world. If I felt regret, the thought of Joe soon wiped it away and I was not sorry.

A week later I waited at the barrier of Peking railway station while the Shanghai train disgorged hundreds of passengers. Security guards still stood there checking passengers as they went through and occasionally picking out this one or that. It reminded me of the day I first came to Peking, nervous and unsure of the future. Yet now I stood in my uniform, again nervous and unsure as I searched the faces for Ni Noo. I was not certain that I would recognize her. I had not seen her since I was six. The only photograph I had was blurred and creased. But when she finally appeared at the barrier I knew her at once. It was as if her ugly pock-marked face had never really left my mind. Unceremoniously I pushed aside the guards as I went up to Ni Noo with cries of welcome. It is not easy to describe the tumult inside me at that moment. Part of it was relief that she had come to rescue my baby from the nursery which over the past few days had loomed in my mind as some kind of Dickensian horror. Part of it was the old need for security and love which welled up as she stood there looking at me as if taking stock of what the years of separation had done. She seemed to sense the intensity of the atmosphere and set out to break it, saying sharply: 'I hope your temper has improved, young madam,' and then she flung her bundle down knelt and touched her head three times on the dirty ground before me, like the slave woman she once was, before the feet of her mistress who had suckled at her breast and taken her love for granted.

It was easy with Ni Noo managing my domestic life. Alan's cook and houseboy left, saying they had not reckoned on a mother-in-law. Ni Noo triumphantly saw them off the premises. I went to work as usual, taking part in the organization's routines of meetings, studies and listening to endless political reports; somewhere in-between I broadcast, interpreted and translated; but all the time happy in the knowledge that Ni Noo was home, loving my baby and running things smoothly.

Several months later Alan returned from Korea to a

domesticated scene, unaware of the conflicts over Joe. He wanted to take a delayed honeymoon and holiday in the popular seaside resort of Peitaho. At first I hesitated. Holidays were only meant for people who were sick and for the foreign experts, but in the end I salved my conscience by taking one of Li Mei's children – a delicate little girl suffering from rickets, together with Ni Noo and little Joe. Alan was philosophical: 'I suppose it's a unique way of spending a honeymoon – two kids and a bloody amah!'

I was leaning further away from Chinese organizational life and if I ever thought I was becoming a 'false foreign devil' it did not worry me unduly. Hsinhua and the radio station helped in making a distinction which brought it into focus when, instead of cycling to the broadcasting studios from Hsinhua as I had done for years I now had a chauffeur-driven car because as the wife of a foreign friend it was considered undignified to cycle to work. When I went to Hsiang Li's home, 'Ber Mu,' my adopted mother, brought me a cup of tea instead of telling me to help myself. I only brought my English husband once to their home for supper and vowed I would never do it again. The atmosphere was so strained it saddened me and I longed for the old familiar relationship. I wanted to say: 'It's me, backward Cheo Ying! I can still make coal balls and unwrap the smelly rags from "Ber Mu's" bound feet. I haven't changed!'

I mourned for the old familiar attitudes but I found consolation in the knowledge that I had Joe, I had Alan and I had Ni Noo and they were mine to love as they loved me.

Now I was married to a foreigner it gave some people in the office an opportunity to vent their xenophobic spite – always there beneath the veneer of a polite exterior – without actually naming anyone through criticizing me. Sammy, who worked in the same office, was deeply resented by many of his Chinese colleagues. He was an adviser on English language but his English was of the Brooklyn streets, not very literate and certainly not of the quality of the Canadian and American Chinese graduates. People like Mark Li resented having their translations corrected by someone they considered educationally inferior and it was not helped by Sammy's lack of modesty: 'Tell that to the boids,' he snapped rudely in his thick Brooklyn accent when Mark and he were arguing over the word 'transport' as against 'transportation'. 'Who's the expoit around here anyway?' Whereas I could like or dislike Mark, Wei Ling and the others when we had our arguments and petty squabbles, I felt free to do so because they were part of our Chinese way of life and to be settled in a Chinese way. When Mark vented his hurt pride on me in criticisms that were obviously aimed at Sammy, I felt hurt that he should place me in the same category as the foreigners and I went to Sammy and told him that it was really meant for him and if he wrote out the self-criticism I would translate it as my own. Sammy told me to choose between being a Chinese or a foreigner and if I wanted to be a Chinese I should look at the criticism and see what I could learn from it. I was so angry I threw a salted turnip at him. He reported me to the office. I was criticized severely for 'striking a foreign friend' and a report was sent up to Party headquarters. The office was in an uproar and this time they sided with me when I refused to apologize under threats of punishment. But how can the Chinese wife of another foreign friend be punished and also save face? I relieved the tension by suggesting that I should also be punished for the first time I had struck Sammy years before when he tried to drag me into his room – a similar situation when he tried the same tactics on Huang Chen's sister-in-law. Sammy hurriedly withdrew his complaint.

Hsinhua and the radio station were eventually split into two separate organizations. Our broadcasting unit, which included Wei Ling, Mark Li, Chang Ching-nien, Greenbaum and myself, moved to a wedding-cake building designed by Russian architects on the outskirts of Peking. It was a wrench to leave all my old comrades in Hsinhua – Huang Chen, Hsiang Li, Scoops. I even suffered Chen Ming-t'ao's embrace and felt as if I was saying goodbye for ever. We were going to join the rest of the international section of the Central People's Broadcasting Station – people whom we had just seen in passing on our way to the studios. Away from the protection and comradely help of my old friends in Hsinhua, I wondered now with Wei Ling and the sinister Greenbaum assuming full control of the English language group how long it would be before I would be standing on a platform with a placard round my neck being struggled against. Already Wei Ling had complained that I was giving too much attention to helping my husband in translating and interpreting and not enough time to my real work. Ni Noo was completely in charge of the boys now. Di Di (younger brother) had joined Joe, and they loved Ni Noo more than they loved me or Alan. It was a wrench to see them run to her for comfort but it relieved me to know that I could work happy in the knowledge that they were being loved by Ni Noo as much as I had been loved by her. Wei Ling and Greenbaum found new ways of making life intolerable. They criticized Alan's reports and accused me of not influencing him to write material that showed China in a proper light. 'Why can't he write about the new bridge instead of about curing syphilis in Tibet?' they complained. 'People will think we are savages.' Now more and more often when we were given political reports at meetings, I was reminded: 'This is not for outside information,' meaning I was not to tell Alan. I often felt my loyalties sorely stretched and wondered how it was going to end as the situation in the radio station became more tense. Wei Ling said to me one day: 'You believe too much in Alan. You are using Alan as a weapon against the Chinese people. He has right-wing ideas. It is your duty to correct his erroneous ideas.' I retorted: 'Why is it *he* is always wrong and *you* are always right? Life is not just black and white, there are shades of grey as well.'

The gap was beginning to widen and I knew that soon I would have to choose what I really wanted to be: Alan's English wife or Cheo Ying with a foreign husband, who was to be made into another Greenbaum or Sammy so he could turn against his own country and parade up and down outside the British Embassy, surpassing even the insults of a Chinese mob. China was no longer the soft, resilient, all-embracing sponge which could absorb aliens and turn them into Chinese-loving friends. It had put up a demarcation line where it wanted its friends to give up their own loyalties to their countries and force them to take a pro-Chinese and anti-foreign line. The softness and acceptance had gone so that one's senses became sharpened into having to decide which side one was on. There was no middle path. In the past I had been made to feel ashamed of my foreign ways and habits, reactions and thoughts, and had been told that they were bourgeois and reactionary. Yet foreign Communists from European and Socialist countries had the same 'bourgeois' habits. Were they reactionary too? As I met more and more visitors from the West I was at first hesitant and nervous of talking to them because there was a feeling of contempt as well as pity for their ignorance. Surely they could see how they were being duped by the capitalists? But gradually I became more reconciled and began questioning my own beliefs in the infallibility of China and all I had been taught and think them rather childish and naïve. I was in the strange position of being able to see my faults and wrong-thinking as a Chinese and at the same time critically see myself as an English girl where the faults were not so terrible after all. It was almost a schizophrenic state of mind. I was not a 'false foreign devil' at all but a 'false Chinese hypocrite'. I had really only paid lip-service to some of the beliefs and attitudes of my Chinese life and the realization dawned that my inactivity in the various campaigns was not because I had a low political level but because they were repugnant to me. It came as a great relief. My misery over Hsiao Mee's fate, the horror of the public executions had been suppressed because I had seen it through Chinese eyes and therefore felt guilt over such un-Chinese emotions. As an English girl it was like a liberation of the spirit to be able to feel loving and kind and to disagree without feeling that it was a political crime.

I longed for the freedom to be honest; honest with myself, honest with others. At all levels of everyday life, there was constant double-talk, sometimes double-think. Each knew that the other was saying things which he or she did not necessarily believe, things which they thought were fashionable or politically desirable, to say at that time. But even close friends could not admit to each other in the utmost privacy that they were aware of the 'We must conform for the good of the Party and of China' game in which they were involved – a game without written rules but with very specific penalties in which everyone was the loser.

At times, one even felt guilty for thinking the 'wrong' thought, for believing the 'wrong' things, for observing facts which did not fit in with the campaign or philosophy of the moment.

When my group during army days had criticized me for my attitude towards my dog they had first expressed sympathy for my tears and then explained how I must not compare what I called cruel standards in China with humane methods in England. 'People in England do not have to worry about where the next bowl of rice is to come from, so they can afford the luxury of caring more for animals,' Wang T'ao had said, and added: 'Remember the RSPCA was founded years before the NSPCC. We have our priorities the other way round.' I had hurriedly written to Auntie to forget my last letter about Hsiao Mee's fate and told her instead that 'it is the revolution which is the most important'. She was not impressed and wrote to tell me so. 'Your Uncle was that upset, he coughed his heart out.'

I was often sent for by the press department of the Foreign Ministry and questioned about where certain journalists had got material which had not been released to members of the foreign press. When I passed on criticisms that foreign journalists made of the press department, it was as if I was the instigator and they were annoyed with me. I could not, like my other interpreter colleagues, ignore or make excuses for lack of proper reporting facilities or deliberately lie about facts and figures. 'Why can't we tell them the truth?' I asked. 'Why can't we just be honest? These people are not enemies of China but in the main want to write about China as it really is. We have nothing to be ashamed about.' Now China had an important position and great prestige they did not want to be reminded of their shortcomings. If a journalist refused to send off their news hand-outs there were plenty of other eager foreign journalists who would. Sometimes when officials refused to give information or facilities I found them by looking through the Chinese press or knowing places of interest.

After the Korean war there were a group of American POWs who chose to seek asylum in China rather than return to serve more years in the army. As propaganda material they were useful but as the fuss subsided they outlived their usefulness and their existence was made increasingly difficult. They were sent to isolated villages and towns where existence was just above subsistence level. They ran away and begged to be allowed to stay in Peking where they could have some contact with other foreigners. Otherwise, they threatened, they would return to the States. 'Let them go, they're of no more use to us,' stated an official of the Foreign Minstry, whose name has since appeared repeatedly in the western press as a prominent Chinese international representative. 'If they don't like what we have offered them, let them go, they can say what they damn well like.' The ex-POWs returned to the States. Foreigners who had devoted years of service to the Chinese cause, helping and training people to take over in foreign languages, medicine and technology, were now made to feel they were of no more use if they did not totally commit themselves to Chinese campaigns and political lines. If they tried to stay they found themselves the targets in anti-revisionist campaigns. Many Americans were in a hopeless situation, unable to return to the States because their passports had been confiscated by their own government. Some managed to seek asylum in the Soviet Union and other Communist countries, while others were branded as revisionists and enemies of China. Those people who had married Chinese partners found themselves in a heart-breaking position. Their children acted as political spies and reported their every word and deed to the authorities. Time and again they were asked to explain innocent remarks they had made in normal family conversation which had been taken out of context. The Chinese partner of the marriage was placed on a platform with a placard round his or her neck wearing a dunce's hat and humiliated before hundreds of people and then demoted to cleaning and emptying the office spittoons. One brilliant Chinese scientist who commanded the respect of scientists all over the world once cried out in agony of despair during a visit to our home: 'They're killing me! What have I done to deserve this?' His death not long after came as no surprise.

We wondered how long it would be before it was my turn. My boys at a Chinese school now came home and shouted more and more anti-British slogans and swore that as soon as they grew up they would kill all American and British imperialists. They were five and six years old. When I

157

explained to them that they were English as well as Chinese they were horrified and screamed and kicked me as if I had uttered obscenities. They ran to Ni Noo and told her to throw these British imperialists out. She looked at me triumphantly and said: 'You see? They are mine, not yours!'

Since I married, Wei Ling's antagonism had become ever more open. It was as if that was the final straw to an intolerable burden. Her own unhappy marriage only accentuated the gap between her empty life and my full one. The most bitter pill was Greenbaum telling his children to call her 'Auntie'. It made me feel guilty towards her and therefore I silently endured her taunts and criticisms. There was a brief respite when she had a campaign against the Americanized Ho Teh, making her life so miserable that Wei Ling was sent off to the countryside for two months 'to help the peasants', while Ho Teh returned to the States, saying to me as she left: 'Now all she has left is you to make miserable.'

Sometimes, when I was reading out a script in the broadcasting studio, I would sense rather than see an evil presence and looking up from my script would find Wei Ling and Greenbaum staring at me with such malevolence that I became nervous and unable to concentrate. At the next meeting they produced notes: 'Cheo Ying sounded bored. Cheo Ying made three stutters.' The criticisms became more sinister and I realized that some of the ideological crimes I was being accused of had sent others to long unspecified terms at labour camps in the North-East. It could only be a matter of time before I would have to go as well. This time there was no Wang T'ao to protect me from the worst excesses of Wei Ling and Greenbaum, who were now on a popular wave of political extremism. Wang T'ao had tried many times to see me after Karel had left but I refused to see him and when I was in hospital having my first baby, Huang Chen had gone to see him and they had had a long talk about my future. Huang Chen always refused to tell me what had been said. As I still hated Wang T'ao I only wished that he would die so that that chapter in my life could be closed for ever.

When I was home I looked at my two slogan-shouting sons and wondered when they, too, would report me to their school for 'wrong thoughts'. If I had any fear then, it was what would happen to them if I was sent away. I knew Wei Ling was insane but while her insanity was centred on me I was a kind of safety valve for her. But the world was closing in and soon the political extremism that was gripping the country would engulf even her.

I began to take steps to leave the radio station before the next campaign, the anti-revisionist campaign, got into full swing. Being married to a foreign journalist, in a climate of growing anti-Russian and general xenophobic hysteria, I would have little chance of surviving. So I decided to ask for leave to further my Chinese studies and do freelance translating work. No time was specified but it was generally understood that it was going to be permanent leave. It was like being expelled from a nunnery. My papers, my badges, all the trappings of a Chinese cadre were handed to a triumphant Wei Ling. It saved face on both sides.

12
Communes

Listening to a well-meaning busybody at the Women's Institute recently reminded me of the women's committee of the
street commune where we lived. The Chinese WI chairman,
followed by her committee members, marched into our house
one day to check whether our establishment was clean. She
lifted up lids from the pots, and said in an aside to her aide:
'Hmn, they've got pork for dinner.' She went on into the
living-room, ran a finger along the shelf to see if there was any
dust and then proceeded to the bedrooms. I had just come in
from work. Ni Noo, followed behind them, her face working
overtime to try to stem my growing anger.

The chairman took her cigarette out of her mouth and said
pointing to a saucer of food left out for the cat: 'That is not
hygienic, remove it.' Then I exploded. Ni Noo tried to get me
out of the room but I pushed her away and told the woman to
get out of my house and not come again without my permission. They backed away astonished. 'We have never been
talked to like that. Don't you know who we are are? We are
the women's committee of the street commune.'

'I don't care if you are Chairman Mao Tse-tung himself,
get out!'

They gaped in astonishment at the outburst and at my
blasphemy. It was beyond their comprehension that they
could receive this kind of treatment from a respected government cadre.

As they hurried out of the room into the garden I shouted
after them: 'And don't smoke in my kitchen, it's not hygienic!'
The woman chairman turned round at the gate and warned:
'You'll be hearing more of this.'

When I returned from the gate. Ni Noo stood trembling

inside the house and admonished me. 'You should not have done that, now we will have all sorts of inconveniences. I shall be regarded as a reactionary element in our study meetings and will not be given any responsible jobs.' Near tears, she added: 'You have achieved nothing by throwing them out. I always knew your temper would get you into trouble. Why didn't you let them look around and satisfy their nosiness? It would not have harmed anyone. It is a wrong attitude to take.' She continued nagging me, regretting my poor English barbarian upbringing after all the work she had put into raising me as a civilized Chinese and declared she was not going to let it happen to the boys.

I sat down at the table, rested my head on my arms and listened to her tirade. I was tired, there were pressures at work and we were in the swing of another mass movement – the communes. I had expressed doubts at the almost frantic speed of communizing land, homes, even livestock in the villages, and the influence it was having on the cities. I had been met with the cold response to 'clarify' my points more explicitly and see whether I had rightist deviationist views. That should have been warning enough to restrain myself, but I had come home with the whole question weighing heavily on my mind only to be met with the commune street committee. I knew I had done wrong and if I did not have misgivings about the whole commune movement I would not have been so rude and insulting to these poor ignorant people who felt they now mattered in our small community.

Ni Noo was right. My treatment had spoilt her chances of becoming a respected member of the community. In her simple sizing up of events was the survival secret – the ability to accept and absorb situations which are alien. Emotion is not allowed to be a natural function. Therefore she was able to rise above any situation and look at it from a purely practical viewpoint.

I remembered a funeral procession going along the road. The mother dressed in traditional white of mourning, was in a pedi-cab, keeping up a moaning chant with tears streaming down her face. The chant and tears stopped suddenly as she turned round to harangue the driver of the pedi-cab behind containing her children, telling him shrilly to keep up; as he caught up with her, she turned back and continued the moaning chant with the tears streaming down again.

During land reform in Huang T'u village I noticed one woman shout and scream at the landlord. As soon as her part was played out, she returned to the crowd, took her baby who had been peacefully suckling at another woman's breast, and continued feeding it at her own, while she calmly watched the next participant in the struggle meeting. Displays of emotion at incorrect times are regarded as signs of weakness and the Chinese become embarrassed. I have heard people describe the Chinese as coldly calculating, but that seems to me just an easy way out of describing something they do not fully understand. It is more a way of life, and has saved China as a nation and enabled the Chinese people to keep their identity despite countless foreign invasions. Emotion is a luxury to be kept in a special box, to be brought out only on special and appropriate occasions.

In political group meetings my reasons for joining the revolution had been criticized as emotional responses rather than political ones. Now, the chairman of the women's street commune raised my bad attitude at the street-commune meeting and questions were asked whether there had been any other examples of my bad attitude towards my neighbours. The old man who kept a stall outside our gate selling sweetmeats and beer recalled that I had swapped him an extremely tough cockerel for a bottle of beer. That cockerel had been a family pet ever since I got him from a peasant at Huang T'u village, which I still visited from time to time. The bird was a fighter and I saved him from the pot after the irate peasant surveyed his battered bleeding flock of chickens, while the cockerel preened himself, putting an occasional feather back into place. 'Let me have him,' I begged as he fetched the chopper. There was something about his independent courage and bravado as he faced the peasant and the chopper as if to dare him to try that appealed to me. 'I'll give you my music box for him.'

So I had returned home on the bus with the cockerel under my arm, wondering what Alan and Ni Noo would say. He crowed all the way on the bus and when I made the last part of the journey home by pedi-cab he crowed again and the superstitious pedi-cab man jammed on his brakes and told me to get off. A cock crowing at midday was bad luck, he said.

When I placed him on the sitting-room floor before the stunned gaze of Alan, he flapped his wings, wiggled his tail and put a deposit on the Tibetan carpet. Then he glared at Alan and pecked at the pattern of the carpet and strutted around. We decided to call him Two-Gun after an American former bootlegger friend who had been bodyguard to Sun Yat-sen. Our Two-Gun lived happily in the garden and in the evenings perched on the window-sill for the night. In the morning, he rapped the window pane and glared if we sat down to eat and had not put out something for him. He regarded the garden as his territory and paraded round all day like some portly butler. He adored the boys, but hated Ni Noo and chased her round the garden and into the house while she screamed for the children to rescue her. It became customary to have one of the boys tagging on to her jacket as she hung the washing while Two-Gun walked round and round in circles fixing her with his eagle eyes.

One morning we found on the high wall hundreds of hens, clucking and fluttering down towards Two-Gun, who carefully served them as they alighted and then marshalled them into some semblance of order. His night and morning crowing had paid off. As we let in groups of angry neighbours claiming their lost hens I decided Two-Gun needed a wife and went to the market and bought him a rather staid fat hen. She settled in happily and together they roosted on the window sill. But two days later she died of fowl pest. Fearfully we waited for signs in Two-Gun. One morning his crow sounded strained and husky. The next day we heard a high-pitched whine and rushed out into the garden searching the sky for signs of a jet plane, but found that the sound came from Two-Gun who was under a hibiscus bush straining to get his crow out. It took all his strength and he ruffled his feathers and looked sad. His fierce eagle eyes became dim and his glorious feathers drooped. We knew it was only a matter of time. He staggered around the garden and even allowed Ni Noo try some Chinese herbal remedy.

'Poor old man,' said Alan. 'The kindest thing would be to put him out of his misery.' But no one had the heart, not even

Ni Noo who could cheerfully chop off the head of anything if it was to be eaten. The old man at the stall offered to kill Two-Gun and put him out of his misery and gave us a bottle of beer in exchange. His end was quick, but that evening as Alan sadly sipped the exchange beer, he said: 'You know, that's the worst beer I've ever tasted,' and poured the rest away.

Now, a year later, the stall-keeper remembered and complained to the Commune that Two-Gun had been too tough to eat and I should have warned him. The local policeman was sent round together with the woman chairman – the perpetual cigarette hanging out of her mouth. We sat in the kitchen and had a friendly argument over mugs of tea. 'You are quite right, Comrade Policeman. To leave food out for the cat is unhygienic, but my anger was not because of that but because of the very unhygienic habit of smoking that Comrade chairman had when she entered the house. I really would like to make a criticism that would help her in her relations with the masses, to be careful where she puts her ash, it is such a bad example to set before the little friends (children) of the commune.'

They left thanking me for my criticism and hoped I would take an active part in the street commune. In turn, I again thanked them for their help.

'Well,' I said smugly to Ni Noo who was looking at me with a sardonic smile on her face, 'I handled that well, you must admit.'

'You might deceive them, but you don't fool me,' she said. 'You did not mean a word of all that.'

The commune movement which started off in the late 1950s and continued through the sixties gave the inhabitants of our particular street a feeling of togetherness similar to the British spirit of the war years. The street was swept clean and regularly sprinkled with water by different households to keep the dust down. The old man who kept the stall outside the gate offered to do our stretch as his stall occupied that particular area and he thought it fair as his customers stirred up the dust and contributed towards the mess. Ni Noo offered to keep the jar outside filled with water. Courtyards were opened up and flowers put out in the lanes. Houses and rooms were shared so that each family had a fair share of space. Nursery play groups were organized and women in different households banded together to form work groups. Children were quick to criticize and report their parents if they were slack in volunteering or took too much living space. They were encouraged to 'help' their parents rid themselves of old-fashioned selfish ways. Our sons came home from school and shouted out slogans: 'Overtake Britain in Five Years,' and then stopping short, puzzled, asked Alan: 'How do we overtake you, Dad?'

Evening classes were set up to teach the majority of people how to read and write. These were highly popular. Literate members of the commune taught those who were not.

The communal kitchen was a flop. There were too many complaints about the food; obviously it did not suit everyone's taste. Though the favourite Peking dish of dumplings had become automated, people felt that the machine could not press the edges of the circle of dough thin enough yet leave the centre thick so as to have a perfectly shaped dumpling. The individual method of hand rolling the circles of pastry was hard to beat.

Gradually families opted out of the commune kitchens and went back to their own home cooking or they were encouraged to share the cooking chores within their own courtyards between several families. Most poor families have individual charcoal stoves which are situated outside under the eaves of their dwellings and so there was never any secrecy about what the neighbours had for dinner. The difference was that now, with the shortage of food in the cities, due to the countryside communes, the whole street knew if neighbours had anything special in the pot and were asked to tell where they had got it from.

The street was involved in all sorts of community problems. The local school became a community centre in a real sense, where children went to school during the day and in the evenings the doors were open to involve everyone in discussing and solving local problems, the care of the old and the sick, children who needed medical treatment and sanitation. They had a sense of purpose and although I deeply resented the prying and lack of privacy, it was my English upbringing that

165

prevented me from accepting the intrusions into my personal life and home. No one had secrets any more. I did not know whether to laugh or cry when the street commune committee suggested to Ni Noo that as a Chinese cadre I should not encourage foreign friends to visit us and if I did I should report to them what we talked about and what their opinions were. Ni Noo, who so fiercely defended my family and would have willingly given her life to protect us, did not hesitate to point out my faults to members of the street committee during the nightly meetings and describe how she would help me overcome them.

Inevitably the busybodies had a field day and caused much unhappiness by interfering and causing domestic strife. A quarrel between the local cobbler and his wife was brought up at one meeting by a neighbour who heard them, and what had already been forgotten was blown up out of all proportion. It ended with the husband slapping his wife's face in public when his patience snapped. He then faced the bigger 'crime' of wife-beating, which could have earned him a prison sentence except that his wife begged that people should mind their own business. She was told the happiness between man and wife is also a commune concern. Some people took advantage of the commune movement to pry into matters that had nothing to do with their normal course of duties. But with the setting up of these urban communes, discussions and criticism meetings were also arranged. One could not be a part-time member of the commune, so all the resentment felt over the Chinese nosey-parkers was soon aired and made known to these women.

There was more resistance to the idea of a commune in the countryside. During the liberation war the peasants had been promised land and now they had land. They had been encouraged a little while later to form mutual-aid teams, which made sense because pocket-sized fields were inefficient. In Huang T'u village the land was sparse and dry. There was very little irrigation and water conservation. There were a few paddy fields but the rice harvest was poor. The main crops were sorghum and maize. Sorghum is a tasteless cereal with very little food value. It looks like purple barley but when boiled it is a light-weight grain which fills you quickly only to leave you hungry a few minutes later. Peasants boil red beans with it to give the grain taste and body. I often gazed out at these parched arid fields and wondered how anyone could possibly make a living from growing food. There was a clump of very tall grey-looking persimmon trees with stark leafless branches reaching towards a bright blue sky. I cannot remember seeing them in leaf but the fruits hung on the branches like bright vermilion lanterns. One fell to the ground and I picked it up to eat. I took a bite and immediately my tongue and lips furred up, making my mouth feel like the dry yellow land from which it grew.

I went back a few times over the years to visit the friends I had made during land reform. The bright young men and women had been sent off to the Workers' and Peasants' University in Peking but most of them had returned unable to keep up the academic pace. As literate peasants they took on administrative roles in their area and were the leading lights in encouraging the conservative-minded peasants to change age-old methods of farming. It made sense to form cooperatives because the peasants could see the immediate advantages of pooling resources and agricultural implements to work their land. Some of the profits were ploughed back into the cooperative but there was plenty over to buy a few luxuries, a thermos flask, sewing machines, even bicycles. In the cottage industries it was better to pool their equipment when making paper, pottery, soap and brushes from sorghum stalks than to do it in their own individual cottages. All these innovations made practical sense because there was material gain, but I was not convinced that the idea of pooling land, communizing all livestock and equipment, would be popular. It was one thing sharing tools and labour, but land, the family pig and chickens was a different matter. I raised these questions. 'Peasants will not be willing commune members,' I flung at Wei Ling during one heated discussion.' 'And don't accuse me of having right-wing ideas,' I said before she did, because I knew that was how she ended all awkward questions. Instead, Wei Ling delivered a lecture, the gist of which was that if there were peasants who resisted the idea of communes it was only because they had been duped by certain elements within the Party itself who were trying to lead China on to the road of capitalism and it was our duty as responsible cadres to convince those misguided peasants; if necessary force should be used.

I was too tired and weak to argue but decided to go to Huang T'u and see for myself. I wrote to say I had a weekend off and could I come to see them. I was welcomed by Shen Ping, one of the peasants who had returned from the university. He was now chairman of the Huang T'u commune. I remembered him as the rather brash young man who had leapt on the platform during a struggle meeting against the landlord, spat on him and then, seeing no one stopped him, had grabbed hold of the cowering man's neck and forced him to kneel and kowtow towards the peasant crowd, banging his head hard on the ground as he did so. Again he had not been stopped so he kicked the now-screaming landlord. Before he went to further extremes, soldiers had stepped in, restrained him and dragged him away from the old man now prostrate on the floor. Shen Ping then turned to the peasants and apologized for his loss of temper, saying he had been carried away by emotion on seeing his class enemy. It made a good impression and he had already started learning the popular clichés – which would help him go far.

Now he stood smilingly welcoming me. He showed me the main office of the commune. It was the former old temple where several young soldiers had so tragically lost their lives nine years before when we were on land reform. Now it was clean, newly white-washed; the inner walls had been knocked down to make a big hall; the paper windows were replaced with panes of glass. On the long wooden table in the centre were several pots of blue hydrangeas. The beaming portrait of Mao Tse-tung with his mole prominent under his lip looked down on us together with the peevish Marx, the serious Engels and the quizzical Stalin. The whole atmosphere was like that of a shrine. There were bamboo covered thermos flasks filled with hot water. The room gradually filled with various officials of the commune and we chatted formally over mugs of tea. I wished I had not written warning them of my coming because the atmosphere was so formal.

The village had changed so much that I hardly believed it was the same place. There were neat clean lanes. Gone were the pigs and chickens roaming at will. The peasants' houses were clean and white-washed with all the rubbish cleared away from the doors. There were no bundles of maize and tobacco leaves drying under the eaves and when I remarked on this, Shen Ping said: 'There is no need, it's all put together.'

'Doesn't that create upsets?' I asked. I remembered that Old Liu – whose house I had lived in during land reform – took particular pride in his own method of curing and his secrecy over the 'special ingredient' he put in his tobacco leaves. We had in those days jokingly said it was chicken manure and pig's urine. 'Oh no,' Sheng P'ing hastened to assure me, 'the commune tobacco is so much better that everyone prefers it.'

The biggest achievement was the abundance of water. There were now huge fields of grain packed so hard and thick that one could almost stand on top of it. Hundreds of ducks were being marshalled down the road to a huge commune pool by a young woman with a long stick with a bunch of feathers at the end. 'They think it's their mother,' Shen P'ing said. The commune was now supplying with force-fed ducks one of Peking's main restaurants where Peking Duck was a speciality. A woman grabbed hold of a duck, held it between her knees and then squeezed a sloppy mixture of ground maize through a tubular piece of cloth down its throat. Their lives were short and I swore I would never eat Peking Duck again.

There were very few people about. I remembered in the old days being surrounded by children and seeing mothers squatting around in groups with a baby suckling at the breast while the younger ones played around their feet, occasionally pushing away the baby from the nipple and refreshing themselves. The mothers barely noticed as they stiched at cloth shoes. The only time I ever saw a mother slap a child was one such sturdy seven-year-old who held tight on to her nipple with his sharp teeth as he turned his head suddenly to see where his friend had run off to. With an exclamation she slapped his face and then shoved her other nipple into his mouth to pacify him when he bawled out at the shock. Now this life had disappeared. Shen Ping elaborated that women were given equal rights. They too worked in the fields and contributed to the wealth of the commune and nation. I wished he did not speak to me in clichés but he was so determined to impress me with the changes since they became a commune that I did not interrupt but listened and looked. I, too, was able to hear one thing and think another. I wanted to know where all the children had gone. He suggested we visit the crèche and kindergarten. The children were lining up getting ready for lunch. They looked at me rather solemnly as they stepped up one by one to have their face and hands wiped by two cheerful girls dressed like hospital nurses. A communal flannel as well, I thought to myself gloomily. Most of the children had red inflamed eyes like the newspaper boy I saw in Peking outside the bazaar.

They sat down and were given a bowl of unpolished rice and a soupy dish of chopped liver and spinach. I felt they were embarrassed by my presence because they tried to look away as they ate and the only sound they made was the noise of their tin spoons scraping their bowls. I went out into the sunshine. I should not have been depressed. The food was better than they had ever had before and except for their eyes they were healthy and clean. There were no ringworm patches on their faces and skulls. Yet there was something missing. Why could they not have all that – and a spirit too? The only difference between the boys and girls was that the boys' heads were shaved in typical peasant fashion while the girls had bobbed hair identical in length. They all wore white cotton pinafores with the name of the commune embroidered in red.

Shen Ping had told me to take a look at the provisions they had made for the aged. 'We house them right next door to the kindergarten so they can enjoy watching the young and feel young themselves.' There were two dwellings, again newly white-washed. One was for the men, the other for the women. 'What about married couples?' I asked. Shen Ping replied that they preferred to be with members of their own sex now that they were old. He told me that my old man Liu was backward in his thinking as he and his wife had refused to join the commune old-people's home and had said so in no uncertain terms. Shen Ping obviously felt that Old Liu was a black sheep of the commune but it made me feel more cheerful and I said: 'Ah well, he is a character, you must admit.'

'A character we can well do without,' was the short reply. In the first dwelling a few old men sat at a table waiting for their lunch. They spoke not a word and did not even raise their heads to look who had come in. The walls were bare except for the portraits of Mao Tse-tung, Lenin and Stalin. A large brassy alarm clock ticked loudly in the corner by a game of chess. In the silence of that room it was as if time was shouting away the last part of their lives.

In the old women's room the old ladies were seated on an enormous *k'ang* – a Chinese bed which is a brick platform heated inside. They sat cross-legged, again waiting; their gnarled work-worn fingers tapped the top of the *k'ang*, a meaningless gesture but so expressive of old people who no longer have any useful function to perform. Shen Ping pointed to their new hats. Perched on top of all the old ladies' heads were identical black velveteen hats with a piece of imitation jade sewn on the front, a Victorian fashion so beloved of old Chinese ladies. 'Their working days are over,' said Shen Ping. 'The commune is showing its gratitude by giving them a well-deserved rest.' Yet the atmosphere seemed to depress him because he said almost as an afterthought that the commune was trying to think of some light work for them to do such as feeding chickens. One blind old lady suddenly cried out again and again: 'My eyes, my eyes, if only I could see!' She was hushed and comforted by the others.

As if to dispel the sudden gloom that hung over us, Shen Ping suggested I see the latest pride of the commune – the methane pit and tank which they had built in order to manufacture gas and pipe it to all the peasants' homes. All the night-soil and animal manure was dumped into a huge sealed pit made from adobe. This tank was painted white; there were various tubes and valves, but very noticeable was a bright red rubber bung jammed in on top. 'What's that for?' I asked Shen Ping. He looked very proud as he explained it was a safety valve and if too much gas built up inside the adobe tank it would blow the bung out.

Some weeks later, during a particularly hot spell, there was a low rumble and a shudder, the tank exploded and the beautifully white-washed peasant dwellings were splattered with foul-smelling sewage. Searching among the wrecked tank, Shen Ping picked up a chunk of clay which had the rubber cork still firmly in place. When I read his letter out to a cynical British journalist, he remarked: 'Now that would have made headlines: "Big Explosion in Chinese Village – Cow Hit by Flying Dung"!'

The commune was not a poor one compared to others because it had many cottage industries; lying close to Peking, this commune was able to supply, apart from the lucrative Peking ducks, paper, soap, pots, brooms and fresh vegetables. But as Huang T'u became more self-sufficient and expanded its industries, it became an almost autonomous state. There was little needed from the city which its members could not produce or manufacture themselves. So the supplies of every-day commodities which Peking depended on peasants to provide dried up as the commune turned inwards. The economy was firmly in the hands of the agricultural com-munes. Food became scarce in Peking and queues built up at the few vegetables stalls; meat was almost non-existent and the cat population rapidly declined. At a well-known Chinese artist's home I had a very passable 'Minority Duck' for dinner once which turned out to be a neighbour's ginger tom.

Goods we had taken for granted now disappeared. Town people became frustrated and angry and there were mutter-ings in the street commune meetings. It seemed as if there was going to be economic chaos. The government introduced rationing of basic foods, while in the countryside peasants re-sented the idea of giving up their personal livestock. The indi-vidual initiative had gone and with their basic needs supplied by the commune there was little incentive to produce sidelines which had brought in added income and alleviated the supplies in the cities. Old Liu must have longed for his old home-made tobacco which made one's eyes smart and brought on paroxisms of coughing – it prompted one dirty-minded soldier to say once. 'If you cough up a round rubber ring swallow quick!' Now old Liu puffed on the bland commune tobacco and calmly waited, keeping his thoughts to himself. What incentive did the women working alongside their menfolk in the fields have now that the making of cloth shoes was done by a special group who had streamlined the whole process? The fancy stitching on the shoes was a waste of time. What had not been considered was the satisfaction of the creative instincts of these women as they stitched exquisite patterns on the soles of the shoes. Their children led well-ordered lives, they were clean and fed and not allowed to have dirty noses. When I saw those red-eyed children at the nursery, I could not bear the thought of seeing more cases like the blind newspaper seller at the market entrance and I begged Shen Ping to discourage the use of the communal flannel. He said very curtly: 'If they all have eye trouble then they can all be treated in one go. Thereby we shall save on the time and trouble of our already hard-working hygiene squad.' Emotion was clearly a luxury which at that time could not be spared. These children were fed, clothed and educated. What right had I to criticize? To try to find a rational answer to Shen Ping I thought of the little slave girl who belonged to a wealthy madame who lived in a house near my childhood home in Shanghai. The madame bought up young peasant girls during famines and if they were pretty put them into her brothels. This girl was too ugly and was kept in the house to work. I remembered her body was covered with little white scars where the madame's pet Pekinese had bitten her. It was a snappy little thing. She slept on a bench outside on the porch with the dog as her only companion. Once the madame called her and, as she stood before her, for no apparent reason the madame stretched out one of her long finger nails and slowly scratched her face from forehead down to her chin. She had to stay there silent until the madame told her to go. Once I gave her a bag of sweets I didn't want, she snatched them and hid in a corner and ate them all. She was like a cowed animal. She did not understand kindness. One day she was found dead on the bench and her body was put into a flimsy wooden box and dumped on the corporation garbage heap. When I remembered that, I felt that by those standards the commune children were very well off indeed.

With such enormous agricultural areas the communes urgently needed giant machines to work the land. The quarrel with the Soviet Union effectively cut off supplies of agricultural machinery suitable for working on these vast prairie-like grain belts. China was still unable to produce enough heavy machinery to supply the demand, so gradually the communes broke up into smaller-sized cooperative-type farms. In the reports and political discussions in the office we were told it was a temporary measure, the step back in the commune campaign into smaller units was not a mistake but useful in preparing the masses ideologically. I said sarcastically: 'Lenin's One Step Forward Two Steps Back' policy. Anyone who thought the speed of the commune movement was much too hasty was heavily criticized and branded as a revisionist. My favourite army general, very popular with all the ordinary Armymen, Peng Teh-huai, was branded and disgraced because he fought against the forced communization of the countryside. The idea had to be implanted in people's minds that this was what would be and the retrograde steps which took place in the countryside and towns were only temporary measures until the time when China's massive industrialization programme was able to support huge communes. The Chinese Communist Party never admit they are wrong. Peasants were allowed to have individual plots of land again, their own pig and chickens and once again supplies began to flow into the city market.

In Huang T'u, after the fiasco with the methane pit, Bulgaria presented a modern fertilizer plant which recycled all the manure and human excrement into high-quality ready to use fertilizer. Shen Ping had written very excited at the latest novelty in his commune.

I decided to have one last visit to Huang T'u before restrictions and other obstacles were put in my way. Already places I had visited on the outskirts of Peking in early days were now excluded to the public. Large areas of the Summer Palace, a favourite spot of the Peking population, was now closed to us and private villas for top officials and visiting foreign dignitaries built there.

I hopped on a bus which took me part of the way to the village, and made the rest of the way on a mule cart. I dropped off by a modern factory-type building. It looked as strange and out of place in that typically Chinese landscape as a farmyard in the middle of Piccadilly. It looked silent and abandoned. I wandered down the lane and found Old Liu with his pig and chickens and went into his house to say hello to his wife. As usual she started off a sentence about her latest grandchild and then waited for Old Liu to finish it off for her by him saying, ' . . . our first grandson.' A ghastly smell wafted from a huge pottery jar which he had in the corner of his heated *k'ang*. It smelt like hot excrement. 'This will be my best so far,' he said, his face wreathed in smiles and his two remaining teeth shining like well-worn ivory. I took his word for it. We had a midday meal of fried french beans and unpolished rice. He had generously invited me to stay because I had brought some Peking delicacies as a present, but I was careful not to take too big a portion between my chopsticks. 'We just take an evening meal in the canteen,' Old Liu explained, as he chucked some bits of food down to the chickens which had run into the house from outside as soon as they heard the bowls rattle. The atmosphere was much more relaxed. Old Liu was happy, his grandchildren came to say hello to 'Elder Sister' and they clambered on to my lap, snotty-nosed and rosy-cheeked as they searched my pockets for sweets. Their mother stood giggling by the door suckling Liu's latest grandson.

Shen Ping arrived smiling, less formal than before because I had not warned him of coming this time. He had kept the piece of adobe with the rubber cork as a memento. 'We were lucky,' he said ruefully, 'just imagine the trouble if someone had been hit by it – a safety valve!' I laughed at the picture and asked about the new fertilizer plant. He stopped smiling and looked serious and sucked in his breath between his teeth. 'I'll tell you something,' he said at last. 'It's broken down.' Apparently the Bulgarians had not done their homework properly. Chinese peasants do not use toilet paper but sticks and stones to cleanse themselves. These sticks and stones had got into the machinery and stopped production.

'We don't seem to have much luck with fertilizer,' said Shen Ping sadly.

The persimmon trees were still there, but there was grass growing underneath with a three-legged pig tethered – a commune curiosity. Trees were dotted around in clumps, the result of the tree-planting campaign some years before. Along the road came the girl with the feather duster marshalling her flock of ducks. The building with the platform where the landlord had stood and been struggled against was still there but was now the commune's cultural centre. There were more trees and flowers and it was hard to picture the bareness of it all just a few years before.

I had my last meal at the Huang T'u canteen and it turned out to be something of a party. Perhaps in our inner Chinese consciousness we all knew that the old days of close friendships was coming to an end. They were no longer the timid peasants of land-reform days when they regarded people like me as the instigators but now saw us as the tools of social change that was inevitable. Stone jars of home-brew, a fiery white spirit made from sorghum which had a smell of rotten straw but was so pure one could put it in a lighter or alcohol lamp, were brought out and our bowls were filled and refilled. We had all eaten dumplings stuffed with garlic shoots and the air was thick and strong with the smell of alcohol and garlic fumes. I remember hazily Old Liu pressing me to try his special tobacco and Shen Ping weepingly describe it as the stuff that came out of the methane pit and not to touch it if I valued my life. Drums and cymbals were brought in and we all joined in the old peasants' dance which was so popular during land reform days, the *yangko*. It went *ch'ang ch'ang, ch'i ch'a ch'ang*, a slow, slow, quick, quick, slow step. Victor Sylvester would have been horrified as we tipsily weaved in and out of the tables.

I was finally piled on to a bus for the long ride home. The moonshine had made me feel on top of the world, the quacking duck that had been pushed into my arms seemed like music to my befuddled mind, and the green droppings it nervously spread around the bus, I looked at with an appreciative eye of an artist and thought how difficult even Picasso would find it to paint such art. I poked my head out of the bus window. 'Shen Ping,' I cried out, 'that methane pit has farted all over the bus!' Old Liu's wife pushed through the window some live river crabs which she had tied securely one on top of the other like a pagoda with moving legs. The bus lurched forward and I cried as I watched their figures disappear in the darkness. 'Be friends,' I murmured to the crabs and duck as I placed them side by side on the seat. I leant my hot face against the cold window and cried. I cried because I was tipsy, I cried because I was leaving them and I cried because I cared.

13

Round Trip

Liu Shao-chi, the now dead former head of state, once told us that all children should be placed in state nurseries to safeguard them from the influence of bourgeois ideas of parents. Our two boys, Joe and Di Di, were taken to the state nursery round the corner from where we lived. Every morning an old man called Pai *yeh yeh* (grandpa Pai) collected them in a little pedi-cart and returned them to the anxious arms of Ni Noo every evening. They learned to sing patriotic songs. With their fellows they were indoctrinated to hate the American imperialists and then came home to play games of war.

'You be the imperialist today.'

'No, I was him yesterday: I want to be the people's soldier.'

The baddies were the Americans and the British, the goodies were the Chinese. I accepted it as part of Chinese life though there were doubts whether it was right to teach children to hate. But I wanted them to be like all other children and was hesitant to be out of step for their sakes.

At the airport one day, to see off a British dignitary, I had the two boys with me. Di Di was eating a sticky bun to keep him quiet. Chou En-lai ruffled his golden curls and asked: 'What are you eating, little friend?' Di Di, all of three years old, replied in a strong Peking dialect: '*Ts'ar P'i Er*' (Fried arseholes). I hastened to assure the Premier that the boy had picked it up from the state nursery where they were having trouble with a spate of bad language among the young inmates.

But he never heard what Di Di had said. He had mechanically performed the duty of a kindly host and such an unimportant detail did not even pass through his mind. He did not have the human weaknesses of the other Communist leaders.

178

He remained faithful to his wife while his colleagues, Liu Shao-chi, Mao Tse-tung, Chu Teh had discarded their elderly wives and married beautiful young women. Chou's wife was desperately ill with cancer and was having treatment in Moscow. Several miscarriages and the hardship during their early revolutionary days had aged her so that she looked more like his elder sister. His charisma permeated those around him without the need for him to utter a word. When I walked into his office at the Foreign Ministry to make the phone call to Wang T'ao many years before, he just stood there and told me not to hurry. Though we still enjoyed the free and easy atmosphere of the early days in Peking I knew that something would develop out of that incident. It did. Overnight the order came that all personnel were to keep to their own organizations unless on business.

To see Chou En-lai at formal banquets and act the charming host delighted his guests but such formalities irritated him. He was not interested in personalities only in people as an abstract political force. An aesthetic who had dedicated his life to theory.

Strangely bad language such as Di Di had used to Chou En-lai was reserved for members of the family and among children's peers. It never came into the children's jargonized slogans condemning imperialist aggression and the Americans. It seemed as if that became part of an arranged order in their lives, for public show. Just as in adult life, the toddlers had their 'official' life and their inner one.

Our family life could have been ideally happy had we been able just to do our work and come home to the children and enjoy normal activities. But that was impossible in China because there was no such thing as a private life any more. We were supposed to be one big family with responsibilities involving every aspect of our lives. It was easy for gullible foreigners to write that they 'could go anywhere and talk to anyone'. All family life was a matter for public concern and control. If we had a group of friends whether Chinese or foreign who were not from our district, the local street committee expected a report from either Ni Noo or myself. Once Ni Noo forgot our ration book and received more than our allowance of eggs and meat. The street committee was informed and she was obliged to make a self-examination in front of her neighbours. One did not talk about one's genuine feelings, except those that one was expected to have. It was a kind of shield, with individual actions guided by slogans and jargonized patter.

I was translating and interpreting full-time for foreign journalists and remained silent at their cynical remarks. We were not allowed to give a definite yes or no to any request or comment, but were supposed to give roundabout answers. The foreign journalists were not very interested in the latest industrial achievements or a new bridge in some far-off province, but wanted 'human interest' stories. 'What's this about clearing up syphilis in Tibet? Is it true 70 per cent of the Tibetan population has veneral disease?' asked one British journalist. He was taken to see a steel and iron complex in Wuhan and then, because he was persistent, to a hospital where they were trying to graft willow sticks instead of steel plates in broken limbs.

I had frequent heated arguments with my Chinese colleagues about the authorities' obsession with showing only the newest and latest developments in China. There was never a reasonable answer when I asked why should we not take these journalists to an old Chinese 'pub' and to talk to the pedi-cab men and labourers instead of only to a factory interviewing model workers. It seemed so obvious to me that there was no danger of the *'lao pai shing'* (the common people) saying the wrong things. A journalist could thus get a more honest and therefore convincing account of life of ordinary people rather than the cliché-ridden patter from chosen workers in factories using the invariable formula: 'Before liberation . . . after liberation . . .' When I took a journalist to a roadside stall and we sat eating and drinking spirits from cracked unhygienic bowls with a ragged man at the same table, the journalist received far greater insight when the man said: 'I was a shit collector before but I'm now a hygiene officer – no one calls me smelly and gets away with it!'

Writers and journalists came and stayed a week or two and then went back to their countries and wrote 'authoritative' books on China. What they had seen was supposed to be 'unique' and the places 'visited by a European for the first time'. There would be a little laughter in the Foreign Ministry Press Department and at Hsinhua because most of these visitors were seeing places and people they were meant to see, and little else. In any case the Chinese people have a special patter for foreigners, so within the limits set by the authorities it did not matter where they went. We soon got used to the circuits given to foreigners in various orders of importance. The commonest was the Shanghai-Soochow-Canton-Peking circuit. In one follow-up meeting when our work with foreign journalists was being discussed I was censured for taking the journalist to the roadside stall. 'You are too *"ma ma hu hu"* (lackadaisical) and do not show a strong enough class-stand. These are our enemies!'

A delegation of MPs came from England to visit China and they went to a famous Chinese beauty spot just outside Peking. One MP nudged one of the Foreign Ministry officials and said: 'I bet this is a favourite spot for courting couples on a moonlight night,' only to be met with the cold reply: 'We do not do such things in China.' The MP, undaunted, replied: 'Go on, you don't get six hundred million people by immaculate conception!' The practice of tight-lipped secrecy about Chinese life was far more damaging than otherwise. When I raised this point at a meeting as an example of the problem facing China in presenting a credible face, I was told: 'What they don't see or hear they can't write about. We must show the good side of China because the bad is not true Socialism.'

I had fought long against being foisted with the revisionist label because it was regarded as such a contemptuous and dangerous thing to be. I was not sure even what it meant and because it was such a term of contempt I refused to accept it. But suddenly I gave in and convinced myself that I must be one because I could not agree with the way my children were being educated. I could not agree with the lack of freedom of thought and movement, could not agree with the way we worked, and as there was so much disagreement I must be a revisionist. Once I accepted the term I no longer felt worried. Like the fear one experiences before the dentist, once the trouble that has been gnawing at you painfully is being treated, the worry disappears and the relief is almost worth the pain. Over the years I had seen decent good people become monsters. They changed from loving, kind and gentle comrades to frightened, furtive characters, determined to stamp out all nonconformity. Too often love, compassion, humanity and warmth were destroyed in the name of that abstract goal of 'working for the people'. Once trying to analyze what 'a good mass-line' meant, I cried out in desperation: 'We are the masses, you and me. We must have compassion, love and concern for each other and not try to destroy each other with political daggers. We are individuals and as individuals it is part of this mass-line to contribute to the life within our own sphere and form value judgements on what we should and ought to do. Our actions should never hurt anybody.'

Mark Li answered coldly: 'That is reactionary talk; we are not individuals but part of a collective and as a collective we must all have one mind. There is no room for individualism.'

If I had remained at the radio station that impassioned speech would have been remembered and used against me in a later campaign.

When I was at the radio station I regularly applied for a year's leave to get my degree in Chinese at university. As each new member joined the group I renewed my request, only to be told, 'Wait another year.' I asked again when I married, pointing out that now I was married to a foreigner I could join as a foreign student at Ching Hua University. I was told: 'Oh no, it would create difficulties among the foreign students if they thought a Chinese cadre had come to join their studies. It would inhibit them.' I could not join the Workers' and Peasants' University either because I had a foreign husband. I was in a position in which I could see my future clearly. I was going to be neither one thing nor another in official eyes but would be designated at whim as it suited my superiors' purposes.

Once during an argument with Alan I threatened to leave him. Alan shouted after me: 'At least wait until you leave China.' I stopped short, puzzled: was that what I wanted? I had never seriously thought of ever leaving China. It had cost me too much to leave what I thought was my home. Alan had taken away the pain of loving Karel and then the two babies had divided my love so that I could not join the pieces and find that something was missing. But existence was becoming increasingly difficult in Peking and though I pushed the thought to the back of my mind the quarrel with Alan brought the whole question of future life in China into sharp focus. I did not want to stay in China. I was too frightened. I had been branded a revisionist. The contradictions within me were becoming too acute.

I turned back to Alan. I could no longer trust my own judgements and see whether they were honest. I wanted to be convinced I was wrong. But it had to be through freedom of speech not by being shouted down with a lot of names which did nothing to convince but which only suppressed one's real thoughts.

I fought within myself. How can I conform if I do not believe that everything the Party and State advocate is correct? Revisionism was an ugly word and once you became tainted with it you were an outcast. So I knew that very soon we must prepare for leaving.

As an interpreter I went on assignments which took me to Korea in the North and as far down as Vietnam in the South, Tibet in the West. But the eastern part of the country had so far eluded me. I knew one day I would go back to Shanghai, the busiest city on the eastern side of China. Unfortunately Shanghai had nothing of news value that merited a special journey there. Unless there was a particular purpose for such a trip, I could not get the necessary official approval. Then reports of miraculous cures by acupuncture and the popularization of Chinese medicine began to make an impact on the outside world. I had always taken for granted that Chinese traditional medicine was best for treating some illnesses and injuries, while at other times western medical knowledge was required. Now with free medical treatment an established fact, the medical services were overworked and overstretched and could not cope with the increasing demand. Large families were no longer encouraged and contraceptives appeared in all the shops where previously they were forbidden. Li Mei at last was able to be sterilized. There were even slot machines for contraceptives. Some of these were antiquated left-overs from American stores and I watched one embarrassed Armyman hit the jackpot when scores of condoms spilled out into the road. Abortions were easy to obtain and

men were encouraged to have vasectomies. I was in an ante-
natal clinic one day when a young woman came to have her
fifth abortion. I heard the doctor patiently go over her case
history and then ask why the various contraceptives she had
been advised to use had not worked. In the end, the doctor
suggested that the woman's husband be asked to come for a
vasectomy. 'It is quite simple,' the woman doctor explained.
'He can come in the morning, just a couple of nicks and he
will be able to go back to work in the afternoon. He will only
lose half a day's work. It won't influence your love happiness
at all.' The woman was hesitant. Exasperated, the doctor
asked: 'Why won't he come?' The answer came back: 'His
mother won't let him.'

Highly improbable cures were advocated for a variety of illnesses. We believed there was a cure for every conceivable
ailment and all that was needed was publicity. We rejected
western medicines and went completely for Chinese cures,
which was precisely what the government wanted as it took
the pressure off the sorely pressed medical services. In the
mass drive for birth control one method advocated was the
'live tadpole system'! A woman had to swallow eighteen live
tadpoles over successive days which would make her temporarily sterile. I tried it out on the cat, naturally scaling down
the number according to her weight and size. She did not take
too kindly to having live tadpoles flicked down her gullet. As
she mysteriously disappeared during the meat shortage a few
weeks later, I never found out whether the tadpole theory
worked. In any case, this system had inherent problems.
First, tadpoles are seasonal, so that it only worked in spring.
So unless the Chinese restricted their sex lives to the tadpole
season it was unworkable. Secondly, many tadpoles carried
the dread disease of schistosomiaisis (liver fluke) and that was
too drastic a method of birth control. I never met any woman
who tried it herself – and I would not advise it. It sounded like
a cure worse than the problem it was supposed to solve.

Shanghai hospitals were reporting medical miracles with
the combination of traditional and western medicine and a
trip was organized for foreign journalists. Fortunately, I was
included. I wondered as we went on the long train journey
from Peking to Shanghai whether I would have misgivings

after seeing the familiar sights which I had kept alive in my memory for so long. Would the experience lead me to decide after all that China was my home? Was there a risk that I would persuade myself that my sense of fear, the lack of freedom of thought were common to millions in China and I should, after all, conform? This was my last chance of ever seeing the place of my birth before we made the final decision of leaving China for good.

When I was a child in Shanghai Ni Noo often took me to Jessfield Park and the zoo. I can remember standing among a group of admiring spectators watching a white peacock spread its beautiful tail. As the crowd gasped at such pure beauty, I said in a loud voice: 'Look at its dirty pink bottom!' Ni Noo hurried me away to see a rather sad black and brown bear climbing up and down the bars of its constricted prison. To punish Ni Noo for taking me away from the crowd whose laughter I knew I had evoked, I played ball with some Japanese soldiers and took their sweets while Ni Noo hovered near-by fearfully. The Japanese soldiers were friendly and as I laughed and played with them I did not realize that China had already been invaded by Japan and that soon it would not be safe for my family either. My sheltered loving life was going to change in a matter of months for the cold unloving atmosphere of an orphanage in England.

But the intervening years in England and then in Peking blurred the memories of my Shanghai childhood until they became disjointed like pieces of jig-saw puzzles from different boxes. Sometimes I thought it was an experience I identified with in a book I had read and stored in my collection of memories as my own and sometimes it was not me at all with the Shirley Temple hopscotch stone, Snow White, the white peacock, the ranging bear, my pet terrapin eating the brothel madame's prize fish, the market place with the decapitated girl's head which blinked and moved its lips, the slave girl and the Pekinese dog; they were a rag-bag collection of memories which if pieced together would make as much sense as a mosaic picture with parts missing. Yet it was those memories, so strong and compelling, that had led me to reject England and come back.

As the train drew near to Shanghai station I felt nothing. A few years earlier I would have been excited at the prospect of seeing the place of my birth. All I wanted now was to re-inforce the memories of the places I knew as a child; it was just to satisfy a curiosity. I went into Jessfield Park, now renamed the People's Park, and wandered into the zoo. There, over twenty years later, with its white tail feathers a bedraggled grey, huddled a bad-tempered old peacock. Inside a building was an elderly brown and white bear. That memory was at least true but what a flimsy framework to have built a life on! Nothing else in Shanghai stirred any memories at all. It was dull, dismal and very quiet. I looked for the house where I lived as a child but saw nothing that stirred my memory. All was lost. Shanghai removed the last vestiges of any yearning I had to remain a Chinese. It was a great relief. There was nothing to hold me any more.

I was called a 'Chink Chink Chinaman' as a child in the Midlands which I took as a rejection. I was called a 'false foreign devil' as an adult in Peking: rejection once again. The first was based on prejudice, the second on a lie. One can live with prejudice but one does not have to live a lie. I was not a *false* foreign devil, I *was* one. An ignorant English girl living as a Chinese was a bitter experience. But China helped me to have pride in myself, to be proud of my mixed blood – the best of both worlds. It made me realize where I truly belonged. All the frustrations and contradictions between my Chinese com-rades and myself were not about politics. My politics were about compassion and empathy for the underprivileged; to the Chinese that was 'bourgeois humanitarianism'. So I could be proud of having a 'low political level'. The battle between them and me was a battle of cultures. Their pressures could not overcome the solid grounding that the Midlands had given me. The coal-miners of Staffordshire, Uncle's silicosis had in their eyes no relevance to the Chinese problems.

'Satisfied?' asked an undersanding journalist, as I tramped along streets vainly looking for familiar sights that would strike some chord of my childhood. I nodded wearily. 'I want to go home.'

Home meant England, not Peking. Alan had been offered an assignment in East Berlin where tension was building up between the two sides and he badly wanted to leave. He felt he had spent too long in China and the old Chinese sponge was beginning to creep into his soul. Berlin was in Europe and as such was westernized enough for us to reorientate ourselves. I was apprehensive about our new life in a strange country. Changing values might affect our relationship. Alan had been my rock in China, my security but I did not know whether the love I felt for him was based on the need to have someone to cling to against a life I could no longer accept or a rebound from my broken love affair with Karel. I still mourned for Karel and the hate I felt for those who had destroyed us was so strong that I had to fight against my own subjectiveness and try to take a balanced view of those I worked and lived with still. The ferocity was so intense that it made me feel afraid that my colleagues would be able to see the distorted picture I was making in my mind and expose me as an enemy of the people. I wanted to get out and yet I was afraid of the outside world because I could never again see it in the same light as when I left it. China does that to people. We learnt to accept our life as it was – unimportant and just dispensible cogs in a vast human machine. Life outside of the collective was not feasible. I was still a government cadre and there was so much red tape to get through. The difficulties seemed insurmountable. I desperately wanted my boys to get out of this world of hate. I did not want them to grow up hating and loving only a man in a uniform because he killed imperialists or loving the pictures of Mao Tse-tung, Marx, Engels, Lenin and Stalin. I was tired of hearing their jargonized patter every time they saw a soldier in uniform: '*Jie Fang Juin Soo Soo Hao*' (Uncle Liberation Army Soldier is Good) and once when we saw a troop train passing by slowly through a road crossing, they waved and shouted repeatedly the same phrase until an open sliding door of a freight wagon revealed the bare buttocks of an Armyman squatting over the edge. With just an infinitesimal pause they shouted: '*Jie Fang Juin Soo Soo P'i Ku Hao*' (Uncle Liberation Army Soldier's Bottom is Good).

I looked at them in dismay. Ni Noo laughed but the boys were quite serious. I had applied for an exit permit and a passport several months before, stating I wished to accompany my husband to East Berlin. What I had planned to do was to make my way to England and register the boys as British subjects. I did not dare do it at the charge d'affaire's office in Peking as I would have had to answer questions of why I, a Chinese official, chose to register my China-born children as subjects of British imperialism. Alan, as far as the authorities were concerned, had no say in the matter.

But the months went by and I was passed from one department to another. In the meantime the anti-revisionist campaign was involving many foreigners who worked in government organizations, and friends close to me disappeared. I grew more and more afraid that the campaign would catch up with me before I could get out. Alan and I in those last few months in Peking threw wild parties as an antidote to the miseries we felt. We danced to rock and roll and invited visiting personalities to join in our frolics. Some came, enjoyed themselves, and then complained to their Chinese interpreters about our bourgeois tendencies. Wei Ling and Greenbaum were still bent on revenge and wrote wall newspapers about my revisionist non-conformist tendencies, and pasted them on our outside walls at night. They also sent a denunciation of me to the security police. I began to develop a fear of everything and everybody, suspecting hidden microphones and tearing up innocuous notes into tiny pieces and flushing them down the lavatory just in case they were misinterpreted and used against me. My terror went to such an extreme that to gain relief I adopted a blasé attitude and thought if I was for the chop the sooner it happened the better. Other times I sweated with fear as yet another one of my friends was held incommunicado, suspected of 'passing restricted information to foreign journalists' and I panicked at the thought of what would happen to my two boys. Still there was no sign of my exit permit.

One evening the answer to all my misery came to me. I would throw myself off the top of the Peace Hotel and end it all. I grew quite elated at the idea. It was such a simple solution. I thought of Wang T'ao and decided to telephone him and tell him. He was in at the beginning, and now it was only fair for him to be in at the end.

I heard his voice again after so many years and I caught my breath at his memory. 'Make sure my sons go with my

English husband,' I said brightly, 'because I'm going to kill myself.' I put the receiver down and went humming into the boys' room where they lay sleeping. Then I sobbed until my chest felt it was going to split with the pain. The telephone rang but I let it ring as I left the house to take a final walk around Peking.

I trod the same route I had walked with Karel that freezing December night when I realized I loved him so much that I was willing to spend the rest of his short life with him in a strange country. I made my way to Pei Hai Park where I had boated in the summer and skated on the frozen lake in winter with Wang T'ao. The park was silent except for the waves of the artificial lake lapping against the marble balustrades. I sat in a moored boat and let myself think of Wang T'ao. Now that I had decided to end it all I could allow myself the luxury of remembering how he had kissed and stroked my body in a gently rocking boat one summer so long ago. His promises, his steadfastness against my wavering weak self, and as I remembered I felt the hatred slowly die away. Wang T'ao loving a Chinese Cheo Ying was entirely separate from the English Cheo Ying and Karel.

'We love you both!' I shouted across the empty lake.

When I returned in the early hours of the morning, the telephone rang again but I ignored it and fell asleep in the chair. At midday the Foreign Ministry sent a message to say that my passport and exit permit would be ready that day. I did not feel any relief. The change from deep depression to the sudden lifting of it happened too fast and I felt a slight tinge of disappointment that what I had planned to do was no longer necessary.

The Russian TU104 took off from Peking airport. I could see my friends just for a second before they completely disappeared as the jet raced the morning sun for Moscow. Out of all my old friends and comrades only Huang Chen had still escaped the net but he, too, would be cleaning out spittoons before the year was old. The others were relatively new friends but they, like him, were caught up in vicious campaigns, humiliated and sent into exile.

Ni Noo cried and screamed on the airport runway, a repetition a generation later of the scene when I was snatched away from her arms, as the boys were torn from her grasp. It is a memory I wished could be obliterated from my mind again. She did not have us any more but she had the street commune and perhaps she would be a more acceptable member now that our dangerous influence was removed. For that I was thankful to them.

I looked across at Alan and we were silent. We were both sad. China had been our home for many years and we had seen it grow from a poor starving weak nation to a powerful arrogant one. So perhaps there should be no feeling of regret in leaving it like this. We needed to change our ideas too because we had become proud and arrogant with it.

As we left the sun behind us I could feel China's hold on me weakening already. It made me feel lost and frightened because I was going to another world with new eyes and understanding. The urge that had coloured and motivated my whole existence in England before was now shattered like some glorious bubble that had burst and I was left in a wilderness. Yet the dawning realization had been building up for a long time, since I first stepped foot on Chinese soil in Tientsin eleven years before. The rebirth was also the beginning of a death – the death of a dream. Don, Wang T'ao, the dog Hsiao Mee, my father, Ni Noo and Karel – my darling Karel – the dead and the dying were just steps towards the final realization that China was not my country after all. My heart and future were somewhere in England.